Contemporary Political Ideas

Derek Heater
Head of the Humanities Department,
Brighton Polytechnic

Longman

LONGMAN GROUP LIMITED
London
Associated companies, branches and representatives
throughout the world

First published 1974
Third Impression 1980

ISBN 0 582 36614 3 (cased)
     0 582 36625 9 (paper)

Printed in Singapore by
Singapore Offset Printing Pte Ltd.

POLITICAL REALITIES
Edited on behalf of the Politics Association
by Bernard Crick and Derek Heater

CONTEMPORARY POLITICAL IDEAS

POLITICAL REALITIES
Edited on behalf of the Politics Association by Bernard Crick and
Derek Heater

Titles in the Series
Parliament and the People
The Cabinet and Policy Formation
Modern Bureaucracy: The Home Civil Service
Parties and Pressure Groups
Local Government
Law and Justice
The Issues of Modern British Politics
Contemporary Political Ideas
Elections
The Commonwealth
Britain and the Outside World
Political Studies: A Handbook for Teachers
Government & Politics of Northern Ireland

Contents

Political Realities:
the nature of the series

A great need is felt for short books which can supplement or even replace textbooks and which can deal in an objective but realistic way with problems that arouse political controversy. The series aims to break from a purely descriptive and institutional approach to one that will show how and why there are different interpretations both of how things work and how they ought to work. Too often in the past 'British Constitution' has been taught quite apart from any knowledge of the actual political conflicts which institutions strive to contain. So the Politics Association sponsors this new series because it believes that a specifically civic education is an essential part of any liberal or general education, but that respect for political rules and an active citizenship can only be encouraged by helping pupils, students and young voters to discover what are the main objects of political controversy, the varying views about the nature of the constitution – themselves often highly political, and what are the most widely canvassed alternative policies in their society. From such a realistic appreciation of differences and conflicts reasoning can then follow about the common processes of containing or resolving them peacefully.

The specific topics chosen are based on an analysis of the main elements in existing A level syllabuses, and the manner in which they are treated is based on the conviction of the editors that almost every examination board is moving, slowly but surely, away from a concentration on constitutional rules and towards a more difficult but important concept of a realistic political education or the enhancement of political literacy.

This approach has, of course, been commonplace enough in the universities for many years. Quite apart from its civic importance, the teaching of politics in schools has tended to lag behind university practice and expectations. So the editors have aimed to draw on the most up-to-date academic knowledge, with some of the books being written by university teachers, some by secondary or further education teachers, but each aware of the skills and knowledge of the other.

The Politics Association and the editors are conscious of the great importance of other levels of education, and are actively pursuing studies and projects of curriculum development in several directions, particularly towards CSE needs; but it was decided to begin with A level and new developments in sixth form courses precisely because of the great overlap here between teaching in secondary school and further education colleges, whether specifically for examinations or not; indeed most of the books will be equally useful for general studies.

Bernard Crick
Derek Heater

Preface

Behind every political action there lurk political beliefs, however loosely held, however ill-shaped, however unconscious their operation. There are empirical beliefs: that the act will in fact achieve the intended result. But there are also doctrinal beliefs: that the intended result should be achieved and can be justified. Whether as motivating forces or as justifications, ideas are a vital element in political life. Thus no study of political behaviour or institutions can be complete without the complementary study of ideas.

The study of political ideas has traditionally been pursued in two ways: the historical and the philosophical, by the study of the great thinkers (Plato, Hobbes, Locke) and by the study of the basic concepts (sovereignty, freedom, power). This book attempts something rather different. I have tried to present the ideas that are potent forces in the world today, drawing examples mainly from the most recent history and treating of the chronologically more remote origins of these ideas in only the sketchiest of ways. Also, examples are drawn from British experience rather more frequently than would be warranted by their importance in a global perspective — for the simple reason that the book is written primarily for a British readership and it has been thought useful to show how the British experience relates to the general world picture. The treatment is analytical. It would have been an easier book to read (and to write!) if a chronological narrative had been adopted. But in a book that claims to be no more than a short introduction, a narrative would have been an unappetisingly thin gruel. My aim has been rather to offer an aperitif to sharpen the appetite.

The order of the chapters and the subdivision of the subject matter are somewhat arbitrary. In practice, ideas are woven into the most complex of patterns — patterns that have been destroyed or distorted by the unravelling process of analysis. However, the human mind must take apart initially in order to understand. I hope that my cross-references will help in some measure in the second stage — that of resynthesising patterns.

Finally, I must thank my friend Bernard Crick for his valuable help and encouragement. He is not, of course, responsible for the end-product.

D.B.H.

1 The Shaping of Contemporary Political Ideas[1]

Political ideas generate lives of their own. They are born in the minds of thinkers who would often scarcely recognise their brain-children after they have grown up under the influences of commentators, journalists and sloganmongers. Our current pattern of thinking has been shaped by fundamental ideas propounded in the eighteenth and nineteenth centuries, remoulded and interlocked by the tensions that have been endemic in our own age. Liberal individualism, social reform, revolutionary Marxism and liberating nationalism are all ideas, which, although still powerful influences today, have their origins in the works of such notable thinkers as Rousseau, Bentham, Mill, Marx and Mazzini in the hundred years spanning the mid-eighteenth to the mid-nineteenth century. By the 1930s, however, the world had become dominated by two pairs of sharply polarised and hostile ideas, each of which contributed the bitterness of ideological collision to the wars fought in Spain and the rest of Europe from 1936 to 1945. The two sets of contrasting ideas that became thus locked in physical battle were democracy and totalitarianism, and Communism and Fascism. Moreover, the situation was complicated by the fact that Communist Russia aligned herself with forces of democracy in the wars while operating a fully fledged totalitarianism at home.

It must not be thought that politics is a closed system, ideas and practice mutually acting and reacting without responding to influences from other spheres of thought and activity. In recent years developments in the fields of sociology, psychology and the natural sciences have had a specially marked effect on political thought. Sociology has held out the great hope that social relations and processes could be understood, explained and manipulated in a manner similar to the achievements that have characterised the natural sciences during the

2 Contemporary Political Ideas

past three centuries. As social scientists have extended the boundaries of their understanding, so political thinking has shifted its focus from all-embracing theories to the possibility and desirability of detailed social engineering. But if sociology has emphasised the potential of applied human reason, psychology has had the opposite effect of highlighting the power of the irrational in human conduct. Psychology has revealed the strength of emotional and subconscious drives that clearly have political implications for understanding individual and mass motivation, thus leading to a certain cynicism about the possibility of reasoned progress that was the major inheritance from the Enlightenment. The immense potential of human reason has, however, been vividly demonstrated by the incredible strides made in this century by the natural sciences — especially in atomic physics, cybernetics and biochemistry — even though the political lessons to be drawn from these advances have been ambivalent. Scientific knowledge means control; but where control over nature means more prosperity, control over man means less freedom.

Since 1945 political thinking has been largely of a negative kind — a record of reaction against the undesirable features of modern society, positive responses being relegated to the flip-side. The thought of the past generation has been dominated by a three-fold fear of war, totalitarianism and the technological society. In August 1945 mankind sighed with a certain relief. A bestial totalitarian regime had been destroyed; but untold human and material destruction had been wrought in the conflict to achieve this; and the war was finally brought to a close by the explosion of the most frightening device produced by man's technological ingenuity. Reaction against war (not just another "world war", but the unthinkable thermonuclear war) has led on to the positive urge towards global cooperation. Reaction against totalitarianism has led to a suspicion of grand theories like racial domination and class war, and particularly to an attempted refurbishing of Marxism stripped of its Stalinist distortions. Reaction to the technological society has not led — except for a minority — to a wish to reverse the trend, which most see as inevitable, but rather to a recognition of the universality of the phenomenon and the need to steer it into directions that will benefit rather than harm or even destroy the human race.

We thus find ourselves in this second half of the twentieth century with a not very serviceable baggage of political mental equipment —rusty tools from a bygone age and dismantling implements from our own. New tools are needed, though this is not necessarily to argue for an all-purpose machine like the totalitarian ideologies of the 1930s. Sir Isaiah Berlin has indicated our requirements:

> The dilemma is logically insoluble: we cannot sacrifice either freedom or the organization needed for its defence, or a minimum standard of welfare. The way out must therefore lie in some logically untidy, flexible and even ambiguous compromise. . . .What the age calls for is not (as we are so often told) more faith, or stronger leadership or more scientific organization. Rather it is the opposite — less Messianic ardour, more enlightened scepticism, more toleration of idiosyncracies. . . .[2]

Technology, total destructive power and global interdependence are utterly new phenomena. Our political ideas must be rethought to incorporate their implications. Tentative and pragmatic this thinking probably should be, as Berlin demands. But a high place must be found on the agenda for a fresh view concerning the relationship between the individual and the state and the idea of sovereignty. In the age of the Welfare state, automation and the Common Market the traditionally accepted relationships just cannot be taken for granted. Each age requires its own particular ways of thought.

2 Mainstream Ideas in Britain

The origins and nature of English parties

Like the USA but unlike France, Britain is frequently referred to as a two-party state — as if it is part of its very nature, as it is part of the very nature of a human being to have two legs. This virtually biological analysis is supported by apparent historical evidence by tracing Conservative-Tory-Cavalier and Labour-Liberal-Whig-Roundhead ancestries. There are continuities in the English party tradition, of course, but twists and turns and realignments to accommodate changing circumstances have made the relationships quite remote. What must be carefully avoided, it must be urged, is any temptation to pre-date the emergence of coherent parties at all. Even if Sir Lewis Namier did go rather far in his attempt to drain eighteenth-century British politics of any idealistic or doctrinal content, he nevertheless rendered a valuable service to historical understanding by warning that the terms Whig and Tory should not be endowed with exaggerated significance or rigidity. Political parties as we know them today — nationally organised and with some semblance of coherent creeds — are scarcely more than a century old. Before that, the patchwork of Tories, Whigs, Radicals, Independents (not to mention Peelites and Irish) gave the British Parliament a decidedly "continental" look.

However, nineteenth-century manoeuvrings did gel into something like a two-party system. Even so, ideological cleavage has been very much less pronounced in Britain than on the Continent, where religious divisions and economic polarities have often hardened into a doctrinal bitterness fortunately virtually unknown in Britain. Since about 1950, indeed, the programmes of the Labour and Conservative parties have been so alike that their welfare policies came to be known as "Butskellism". We might similarly dub the frantic search for economic stability in the decade following the Labour Party victory in the 1964 election as "Heathsonism". A reduction in class tension; the need of both parties to woo trade unions and employers; competition to secure voters from "the middle ground"; increased importance of bureaucratic and technocratic expertise — all these factors have tugged Conservative and Labour towards each other until "two monolithic structures now face each other and conduct furious arguments about comparatively minor issues that separate them."[1]

> Yet for all this agreement there was between Tory and Socialist a conflict over the meaning of the party system, the constitution, and democracy itself that one might well call fundamental [writes Professor Beer]. . . . I conclude that in practice as in theory, in the actual distribution of power as in their reigning conceptions of authority, the two parties were deeply opposed.[2]

And it is to this deep opposition that this chapter is mainly addressed — to an investigation of Conservatism and Socialism British-style. For, even in Britain political parties may in many ways be viewed as institutionalised ideas. But, we must also take a brief look at Liberalism — a Victorian and Edwardian left-over, but still an important strand in our political thinking for all that, with an influence beyond its mere party-political strength. It is convenient to examine the Socialist tradition first.

Democratic Socialism: the context

Democratic Socialism — in the residual sense of class-consciousness, economic planning and egalitarian social reforms — has been the most conspicuous programme in the post-war world even outside the Communist network of states. Turning aside from the stern revolutionary route of Marxism and following the parliamentary reformist path trodden in the late nineteenth century by Bernstein and the Webbs, exponents of the doctrine have used it as an invaluable *vade mecum* in both Western Europe and the Third World — both overtly Socialist governments and also politicians (like the Christian Democrats) belonging to quite different traditions.

After 1945 in the six countries that came to form the Common Market, Socialist parties vied with Christian Democrats for power; while in the Scandinavian countries Socialist parties were even more powerful. State planning of the economy, bolstered by the urgent need for rehabilitation after the ravages of war, became an accepted principle, typified by Monnet's great creation, the *Commissariat au Plan,* in France. Planning was swiftly followed by economic prosperity, which in turn was transmuted into social welfare programmes. Even in the USA, that most capitalist of countries, social welfare policies had come to be accepted as desirable by the Democratic party by 1960. Kennedy proclaimed the New Frontier, the necessary legislation for which was left to his successor's Great Society Programme.

However, the most self-consciously socialistic politicians in the post-war decade were the great leaders of the emerging Third World, especially that alliterative quartet Nehru, Nkrumah, Nasser and Nyerere. Nehru undertook a daunting programme to transform India into the largest democratic socialist country in the world under the twin influence of Webbite planning and Tolstoyan pacifism. In many countries socialism was almost synonymous with nationalism: expropriation of the wealthy meant expropriation of the great international companies that held so much power in their lands; a fairer distribution of property meant a more egalitarian society; renunciation of the imperial regime meant, in Africa at least, a revival of communal, tribal traditions. Thus Nasser: "In dealing with feudalism our aim was to transform tenants into owners. Thus we shall have a socialist, democratic, cooperative society."[3]   And Nyerere: "In traditional society everybody was a worker.... Even the Elder ... had, in fact, worked hard all his younger days.... One of the most socialistic achievements of our society was the sense of security it gave its members, and the universal hospitality on which they could rely."[4]

So, when the Attlee government introduced its impressively widespread programme of socialist legislation it was not, at least in the long term, a unique operation. This is not to say that there are no features of the British Labour movement that distinguish it from other Socialist parties. Before analysing its general socialist doctrine in operation, it will indeed be as well to sketch in some of the particularities that have shaped the development of the movement.

The Labour Party evolved haltingly at the turn of the century as a coalition of disparate pressure groups concerned with the lot of the working class. Its intellectual and emotional roots are equally diverse. Pledged to the achievement of Liberty, Equality and Fraternity in an industrial context, it has often been noticed that the Christian tradition of fraternity is a stronger strand than the socialist tradition of egalitarianism: Methodism more than Marxism. Indeed, the Marxist emphasis on class antagonism was considerably watered down by the Fabians – a society founded largely on the initiative of George Bernard Shaw and Sidney and Beatrice Webb in 1884, and which, preaching "the inevitability of gradualness", has had a deep influence on the thinking and action of the Labour Party. A pragmatic reform of social conditions rather than doctrinal Socialism. Indeed, the party did not adopt Socialism as its official creed until 1918. Three great figures dominated the thinking of the Labour Party during the generation following 1918: G.D.H. Cole, who emphasised the need to increase the workers' control of industry; R.H. Tawney, who emphasised the importance of social equality; and Harold Laski, who emphasised the significance of class conflict.

Because of the different emphases and interests of the membership, and because of its dual pragmatic and ideological origins, the party has been prey to dissension between fundamentalists (who wish to adhere to Socialist dogma) and revisionists (who wish to adjust policies to circumstances) – a problem that plagued it especially in the 1950s. Furthermore, it has suffered a more severe electoral weakness than would otherwise have been expected because of the so-called deference vote – the forelock-tugging propensity of large segments of the English working class to vote for their "betters" rather than their "mates". Since 1945 something like half the Conservative vote has come from the working class. However, to counterbalance this disadvantage, it must be remembered that the Labour Party is virtually the sole left-wing party in Britain. Unlike the French socialists, for example, it does not have to share the left-wing vote with a vigorous and popular Communist party.

Labour Party doctrine

The basic concept of socialism is the belief that politics is about class: that the social privileges of the middle class and the economic deprivation of the working class are unjust and present a challenge to reformers; that the rectification of this imbalance is the prime function of politics. Although clearly class dissension does not display the same acrid bitterness that characterised British society in the 1920s, it is the belief of a number of acute observers that the force persists – irrational and obsolete though it might be in this socially more mobile age. Thus the late Professor Hanson, writing after the 1970 election about the two major parties, declared: "It is true that... their respective class-identifications have become less clear; but no change recognisable as qualitative has yet occurred." [5] The American scholar, Samuel Beer, suggests that the concept of class is in the very bloodstream of Britain: "In a country such as Britain, where class feelings are so ancient and deeply founded, it is hardly implausible to suggest that quite apart from what rational self-interest may dictate and leaders may try to impose, the sense of class irresistibly demands political expression."[6]

How has this fundamental assumption of the class basis of politics affected Labour Party thinking? It has had two broad influences: on the party's general thinking about political activity and on specific programmes. Now it must not be thought that the Labour Party, even in its most aggressively ideological moods, has looked forward to a class war in a Marxian sense. There is certainly nothing so blatant in their election manifestos. Rather has the belief in the reality of class divisions given the Labour movement a sense of cohesion and righteousness which it would otherwise have lacked. However strained the pretence might become on occasions, the Labour Party likes to emphasise its sense of comradeship in preference to its search for power, because, whatever their social origins, all members of the movement are united in their single basic goal of improving the lot of the working class.

Their fundamental ideal or goal is equality. If anything, increasing weight is being placed upon this aspect of the party's doctrine. Hugh Gaitskell declared quite unequivocally in 1958, "The central socialist ideal is equality. By this I do not mean identical incomes or uniform habits and tastes. But I do mean a classless society ... one in which though people develop differently, there is equal opportunity for all to develop." [7] This kind of classless equality can be achieved only if advancement is based on skills rather than birth, and only if skills can be nurtured irrespective of birth or wealth. Much of this boils down to the abolition of distinct forms of education and the provision of a universal state system that will develop each individual's potential to its maximum. And the educational programmes of the manifestos indirectly reveal the class basis of Labour politics. "The widening and extension of education", declared the 1970 manifesto, "is ... the best way of developing a society based on tolerance, co-operation and greater social equality. The education system itself must not perpetuate educational and social inequalities." [8] Education is the great class tool, but it is two-edged — it can shape either a stratified or a classless society.

However, when the Labour Party established its first majority government in 1945, the major issue was the public ownership of industry. Clause IV of the party constitution pronounces:

> To secure for the workers by hand or by brain the full fruits of their industry and the most equitable distribution thereof that may be possible, on the basis of the common ownership of the means of production, distribution and exchange and the best obtainable system of popular administration and control of each industry and service.[9]

The election manifesto of 1945 provided a meticulous list of the industries to be nationalised; yet nationalisation was conspicuous for its absence by 1970. Why was the issue so important in 1945? Why did it decline in significance? (Since this was written interest has revived.)

For most Labour Party members in 1945, and still for the fundamentalists in the 1950s, capitalism represented an evil economic system founded upon the socially immoral principle of competition. A truly socialist society could not be established until competition was replaced by cooperation as the economic motive force; and this, it was argued, could only be achieved by public ownership replacing private. Moreover, public ownership was believed to be essential if the economy was not to develop in an intolerably haphazard way. Nationalisation was an absolutely essential precondition for effective planning. This major article of faith was realised in the great programme of nationalisation undertaken immediately after coming to power in 1945. But, the faith soon faltered. Aneurin Bevan and the left wing of the party fought for the principle: there was a bitter struggle over the retention of Clause IV in the party constitution in 1960. "The 'ghost' [of nationalisation] haunted the party of the 1950s because it had been the soul of the party in the 1920s and 1930s." [10] But by 1950 it was a ghost — or rather a noisy poltergeist — an insubstantial shadow of the past, not the substance of present reality. Why the fading of interest? There are two major explanations. Firstly, the particular system of public ownership that was used brought little change in practice from the former system of private companies. The workers were merely working for new bosses who operated the industries in the old way; many of the nationalised industries, like transport and coal, were in decline and could hardly be expected to run without incurring financial losses; and it came to be realised that *control* could effectively be exercised without the embarrassment of *ownership* (a distinction put forward by Anthony Crosland). In short, there was disillusionment: nationalisation did not bring the Socialist Commonwealth. The second reason was the cool attitude of the trade unions — a powerful influence in the councils of the Labour Party. We have already noted the close interconnection between nationalisation and planning. But planning, of course, means diversion of manpower and wage and price controls; neither of these measures was palatable to the trade unions, who were content with the Welfare State reforms but remained jealous of their freedom to bargain for the sale of their labour.

Nevertheless, although nationalisation is now diminished in importance as a Labour Party doctrine, planning is still very much a live principle, a principle that distinguishes Socialists from Conservatives probably more than any other issue. "For the Conservatives," said Harold Wilson in 1960, ". . . the role of the state is confined to guiding, influencing and holding the ring. . . . [For the Labour Party] the commanding heights of the economy should be . . . answerable to the community and working in its interests." [11] There are a number of reasons for this creed. Firstly, there is the recognition, already present in the interwar years, that complex modern industrial society consists of a number of closely interrelated parts. Control of one part — by the nationalisation of the railways, for example — would, it is believed, be only very partially successful unless other components of the industrial complex are welded into a plannable whole. Secondly, the Labour Party argues that if resources are scarce then planning is essential for a humane distribution of the goods and services that are available: individualism must be replaced by fellowship. However, planning is not merely a policy for an emergency, like wartime rationing. Socialists believe that planning, if anything, is all the more important to encourage the production and just distribution of abundance. Clement Attlee made this quite clear in a letter to Harold Laski. He wrote: "The acceptance of the doctrine of abundance, of full employment and of social security requires the transfer to public ownership of certain major economic forces and the planned control in the public interest of many other economic activities." [12]

A planned economy may be achieved by either physical planning or by economic management — by direction of labour or by fiscal manipulation. Except for a short two-year period immediately after taking office in 1945, planning by Labour governments has been of the fiscal kind. By tinkering with the bank rate, adjusting indirect taxes even imposing import quotas and a statutory freeze on wage increases, Labour ministers have tried to direct the economic currents to carry them through their government's social programme rather than be swept along themselves by the eddies. The switch in policy was illuminated by the "bonfire of controls" ignited by the President of the Board of Trade, Harold Wilson, in 1949.

Since then there have been three phases in Labour's planning policy. First, there has been the "discovery" of science and technology. [13] And, as it promised in its 1964 election manifesto, in Part 2: Planning the New Britain, the Labour government set up a new Ministry of Technology (Mintech) "to guide and stimulate a major national effort to bring advanced technology and new processes into industry". [14] Rather like Thurber's grandmother, who thought electricity was leaking out of the empty light-socket, the Labour Party envisaged the power of modern technology going to waste unless harnessed by effective state planning. Then came the era of immense activity. Extra civil servants were recruited and special economic advisers were drafted in to Whitehall after the creation of the Wilson administration in 1964 – to man the Prices and Incomes Board and the Department of Economic Affairs; to draw up George Brown's National Plan; to revivify the development areas. All was bustle. But Labour brought forth a mouse, the mountain of planning defeated by the government's failure to achieve economic growth and to discipline the unions. And so, although planning was emphasised in the third of our phases (the 1970 election), it was placed in the context of a mixed economy rather than government direction:

> It is our purpose [declared the 1970 manifesto] to develop a new relationship with both sides of industry, in which the forward plans of both Government and industry can be increasingly harmonised in the interests of economic growth. In the public and private sectors, industrial enterprises are paying increasing attention to medium and long term planning. [15]

We are all planners now – so the message might read. Similarly, it could be cogently argued that the welfare state is now accepted by all. Nevertheless it was Socialist in origin. The idea of social welfare provision was certainly the major theme of Labour Party policy from about 1946 to 1960 — from the euphoria over the National Health Service to the flirtation with affluence-through-technology.

In 1945 it would be difficult to say which was considered the more important — nationalisation or welfare state. But the policy of social welfare came to the fore because of trade union pressure and the disillusionment of both unions and revisionist intellectuals with nationalisation. The ordinary man-in-the-street or on the shop floor was more interested in insurance against sickness, unemployment and old age than in who was his ultimate employer. And since in any case as we have seen, nationalisation proved not to be the panacea that had been fondly hoped, the revisionists of the 1950s started talking in terms of social equality (i.e. welfare state) as being the ultimate Socialist goal, while public ownership was relegated to being merely one of a number of means which would be employed interchangeably depending on conditions and their proven efficiency.

As late as 1959 the welfare state was the keynote of the Labour election campaign — the businessmen may never have had it so good, but what about "the widowed mother with children, the chronic sick, the 40,000 unemployed, and the millions of old age pensioners who have no adequate superannuation"?[16] Such was the challenge of their manifesto's opening paragraphs. By 1964 that message was already muted, drowned in the technological planning cadences just described. The trouble was, of course, the Tories had stolen Labour's welfare clothes and Labour could not afford the more expensive garb of universalism: Tories and Socialists alike had to wear the modest welfare apparel of prescription charges and the like, the one by choice, the other out of financial necessity.

Humanity and justice, the respect for the dignity and needs of the individual, have not been confined in Socialist thinking to the national plane. Indeed, Socialism has traditionally been proud of its internationalism. Peace and international security rather than nationalist flag-waving has always been the Socialist style. For example, at the height of the Cold War, R.H.S. Crossman could write about the change from a situation of European ascendancy to the Washington–Moscow bipolarism and assert that "The task of socialism is neither to accelerate this Political Revolution, nor to oppose it. . . , but to civilise it. To do this we must realise that a victory for either side would be a defeat for socialism."[17] In 1960 occurred the famous Scarborough party conference when Gaitskell came under heavy pressure to accept a policy of renouncing Britain's nuclear weapons. Part of the pressure on this issue was generated by the CND movement; and it must be recognised that Labour is held to be more responsive than the Conservatives to grass-roots pressure groups of this kind. One of the main peace-keeping forces in the world is the United Nations Organisation and it is not surprising that Labour politicians have been at pains to declare their support for its work, especially the activities of its Specialised Agencies against the ravages of disease and poverty. Ever since 1945 the speeches of Labour politicians from Bevin to Wilson, election manifestos too, have denounced the evils of world poverty and have pledged the party to its alleviation. The Ministry of Overseas Development was established by the Wilson government.

Closely allied to the problems of underdevelopment are the issues of race and Britain's relations with the rest of the Commonwealth. Again, the declared tradition has been a liberal one — discouraging discrimination and encouraging the continuation of the Commonwealth as a multiracial organisation. Support for the Commonwealth, indeed, even led Gaitskell and Wilson into anti-Common Market stances.

There is much in the above account of Socialist internationalism that might seem to accord ill with the practice of Labour governments. The "Bomb" has been retained; negotiations were entered into with the racialist regime in Rhodesia; financial allocation to overseas development was cut — and so the list of paradoxes might be continued. One must question, therefore, in this field, and indeed in all the others, whether the Labour Party has recently lived up to its Socialist pretensions.

Is the Labour Party really socialist?
The history of the Labour Party since 1945 may well be viewed as a whole series of strategic withdrawals from prepared ideological positions: from public ownership to welfare state; from welfare state to planning; from planning to humanitarian reforms; from humanitarian reforms to schemes for rendering capitalism effective — a retreat which has taken the party from Socialism to pragmatism. Is this a fair appraisal?

In 1945, the party firmly declared: "The Labour Party is a Socialist Party and proud of it. Its ultimate purpose at home is the establishment of the Socialist Commonwealth of Great Britain." [18] For a generation after the 1918 commitment to Socialism the party remained doctrinally united — committed to the realisation through considerable legislative activity of a fully socialist society. By 1947-48 this cohesion and commitment was becoming seriously undermined. Disillusionment dawned with the difficulties. And the change, of course, was signposted by the shift from an attempt at management by direction of manpower to management by fiscal manipulation. How can one explain this change of heart? A number of factors contributed, such as the reduction in class tension and the increasing affluence of the 1950s. But there is perhaps a more deep seated reason. Professor Beer is of the opinion that "The adoption of Socialism as an ideology was functional to this choice of political independence [from the Liberals in 1918]. If the party was to pursue power independently, it needed a set of beliefs and values distinguishing it from other parties." [19] By 1950, however, the Labour Party had tasted independent power: it no longer needed to protest its dogma quite so vociferously.

And so came the period of revisionism. Not a rejection of ideology so much as the search for a new one. But in readmitting market control of the economy, the revisionists readmitted the principle of competition instead of the basic socialist doctrine of cooperation. Socialism was by that much undermined.

It was but a short step to Wilson's new definition:

> Socialism, as I understand it, means applying a sense of purpose to our national life: economic purpose, social purpose and moral purpose. Purpose means technical skill ... in Government and in business we are still too often content to accept social qualifications rather than technical ability as the criterion. [20]

Socialism is now mere technique, or pragmatism as Mr Wilson has termed it. Gone are the days of the blueprints. Issues must be dealt with as they are raised by the best technical skills available. Many Socialists have felt the cause betrayed and have called for a rallying to a New Left who will be faithful to the Socialist tradition. [21] But most radicals still support the Labour Party as the most likely vehicle for social reform such as comprehensive education, and humanitarian reforms such as the abolition of capital punishment, even if in economic terms it is merely trying to create a capitalism with a human face.

Conservatism as a negative doctrine

Just as Socialism contains a positive urge to bring about change, so Conservatism contains a wary suspicion that change might be ill-considered. This defensive posture can be traced back to the time of the French Revolution: it is necessary to defend the status quo against the frenzy of change and revolution. Edmund Burke, the Irish father of English Conservatism, preached the doctrine of conservation and continuity against what he believed to be the counter-productive violence of the revolutionaries. And since his early, hypothetical fears were substantiated by the excesses of Jacobinism, his ideas won much favour in England in the 1790s. In fact, the continental countries were more directly threatened by the disruption of revolution, and Conservatism as resistance to change became hardened more solidly there than in Britain in a system identified with the name of the Austrian chancellor, Metternich.

This interpretation of Conservatism as a response has a number of shades to it. Defenders of the position, like Lord Hailsham, view it as a positive virtue: most attempts to change society are either evil or misguided and the Conservative must therefore stand sentinel over the hard-won values of life.

> The most a politician can do [he has written] is ... to prevent fools or knaves from setting up conditions which make any approach to the good life impossible except for solitaries or anchorites. ... [The Conservative Party's] eternal and indispensable rôle is to criticise and mould the latest heresy of the moment in the name of tradition. [22]

But even if this extreme position is not adopted, defence of the status quo is still rated more highly than change, at least of a rapid nature. Reform must be controlled and be a remedy for specific ills. Opponents of Conservatism, on the other hand, interpret this pragmatic response style of politics as evidence of intellectual hollowness. Incapable of generating any positive ideas itself, Conservatism acts only when stimulated by hostile and provocative mental prods.

The status quo that has to be defended, the stimuli that have to be responded to, change from time to time. This circumstance may lead Conservatives into the appearance of being trimmers, of changing course for the sole purpose of retaining power for its own sake. This impression is moreover strengthened by their self-confident claim to be the natural governors, identified as such by birth or talent. Since Burke's revulsion against the French revolutionary experiment with democracy, Conservatives have mistrusted the placing of political power in the hands of the masses because of their inexperience and fickleness. In the nineteenth century, Disraeli was to reiterate this sentiment in his plea for the preservation of gentlemanly, aristocratic values in a brash industrial age. The view of Conservatism as merely a pragmatic response to circumstances is further reinforced by their refusal to draw up a detailed legislative programme as a chart for the government once elected. In the words of the admittedly biased commentator, the Labour politician Peter Shore, "it is a distinguishing feature of Conservatism that it has no social goals to achieve, no major changes to make. It follows from this, and experience demonstrates the truth, that Conservative Governments are seldom memorable for their legislation; they are almost wholly concerned with administration." [23]

The positive features of Conservatism

The negative doctrine — whether the active style of resistance to ill-considered change or the passive style of holding on to power without disturbing the status quo — by no means fully explains Conservatism. A wide range of politicians have, in fact, woven a complex pattern of theory to explain the meaning of the movement of which they have been distinguished members — Edmund Burke, Robert Peel, Benjamin Disraeli, Randolph Churchill, Quintin Hogg. Three major motifs may be discerned in this pattern: the theory of the organic state, respect for law and authority, and the subordinate role of politics. To understand the positive features of Conservatism we must examine each of these in turn.

The two main analogies used in writing about the state are a machine and a living organism. The Conservative firmly believes in the latter. Society has a life of its own, exists as something more than the sum total of the individuals of whom it is composed. Like a being endowed with life, society is not constructed to an ideal plan; it must change, grow, evolve. Moreover, the various organs of this being — the groups, classes and interests — must work in a coordinated way; to posit, as the Socialist does, a condition of hostility within the body politic, is to expound a contradiction in terms. The Conservative therefore speaks of national unity. After five years of the Attlee government, the Conservatives declared that, "by partisan measures and factious abuse, the nation has been deeply divided in the last five years. A Conservative Government will set itself the task of bringing the people of Britain together once again."[24] In the same vein, Mr. Heath reiterated the slogan, "one nation". The Conservative view of class is, in fact, quite contrary to the Socialist — integrative not divisive, providing social links and relationships not inciting social enmity. Disraeli wrote of the existence of "two nations". But his aim was not to retain their hostile stance (this, he believed, was the unfortunate effect of complacent laissez-faire liberalism), but to reunite them in mutual recognition of their respective rights, places and functions. What is more, class co-operation has been no mere abstraction: while Prime Minister, Eden advocated "partnership in industry" as a relationship very much to be encouraged.

The most familiar feature of Conservatism's organic theory is its emphasis on tradition and continuity, expounded classically in Burke's more-in-sorrow-than-in-anger *Reflections on the French Revolution.* What has stood the test of time is good and must not be lightly cast aside. Indeed it is more than good, it is natural: "To preserve the method of nature in the conduct of the state — because nature, as Burke observed, is wisdom without reflection and above it: this is Conservatism." [25] A nation's heritage must be cherished and it is the politician's solemn duty to ensure this. A grandiose conception preached by the philosphers, though none the less sincere and valuable for all that. For the more mundane, the preservation of tradition means the comfort of orderliness and of the familiar.

For the landowners and gentlemen among the Conservatives, preservation of traditional values has a particularly high priority and may almost be enough in itself. But there are and have been businessmen and professionals in the Conservative ranks as well. And for them the preservation of the traditional does not mean stagnation. What is stagnant is dead — not a living organism. Conservatives do not believe that the ideal is attainable but they do believe in development and progress. Thus could Macmillan boast that Britain had never had it so good and the Bow Group press within the party for progressive social reforms. In distinction to the Socialist theory of reform, however, progress is seen by the businessman type of Conservative as the outcome of encouraged enterprise, not enforced egalitarianism. Energy and drive are the virtues to be extolled; the successful private businessman, the model to be copied. "We plan", announced the 1970 manifesto, "to hand back responsibilities wherever we can to the individual, to the family, to private initiative, to the local authority, to the people." [26] People must learn "to stand on their own two feet", declared Mr. Heath when he became prime minister; business concerns that were "lame ducks" would not be helped by government subsidies.

Belief in the country as an organic whole, the cherishing of traditions, the rejection of the idea of class struggle — all lead on to a heightened sense of patriotism and national self-consciousness. From 1964 to 1970, writes a professor and former Conservative M.P. "we became strikingly civilian-minded and disturbingly insular." [27] The Conservative reading of history is that Britain has been a great country in the past and their concern is that Britain should cut a fine figure in the world today. Conservatives are not ashamed of pride.

As each organ in the body has its appropriate place and function, so every group in an organic society has its due role; and as the brain commands the muscles, so the governing elite must command the lower classes. The concepts of law and authority are consequently major features in Conservative doctrine. Moreover, law and authority are viewed as more than man-given; they fall rather into the natural order of things, an order which for many Conservatives has an essentially religious foundation. Law must be respected — but only if it is a just law, based, as Burke urged, on judgment matured by an understanding of the society's traditions, not on the fallible whim of the uninitiated legislator.

Respect is due to duly constituted authority. This respect is not only natural, it is also necessary for a strong, stable and efficient government - very desirable qualities for the Conservative. "What Britain needs," announced Mr. Heath in a speech in 1969, "is bold government, strong government, stable government. A Government prepared to tackle the problem of strikes and of restrictive practices. A Government prepared to tackle the problem of a penal tax system. . . . Above all, what we desperately need is not more government but better government." [28] The Conservatives use the state paternally, Socialists fraternally. There is therefore a distinction between rulers and ruled: society must be constructed hierarchically. Rulers rule. That is their function, indeed their duty. Government is an art, a specialist vocation, requiring particular skills and qualities which are not distributed widely about the community. Government must consequently be in the hands of an elite. *Noblesse oblige* — power is the duty of the privileged. But no longer is the privilege of birth considered the necessary hallmark for leadership, rather the privilege of individual merit — the Tory Democracy as expounded by Randolph Churchill. Even within the party there is hierarchy, unlike the intraparty democracy of the Labour Party. The party leader has a more exalted position. If his personality outshines the rest of the party — be he a Disraeli, a Churchill or a Supermac — so much the better. But in any case, policy is in his hands. Election manifestos, for example, are couched as personal statements to the electorate. The leader has the prerogative of and responsibility for drafting policy. He is trusted to do this. The Conservative Party therefore places less reliance than the Labour Party on agreed detailed programmes. Once the government has been elected, it must be left to undertake the task to the best of its ability without being tied to mandates or promises: "A British government ... is an independent body which on taking office assumes the responsibility of leading and directing Parliament and the nation in accordance with its own judgement and convictions." [29]

The exercise of leadership and authority means that the Conservatives do not shun the idea of a managed economy, even though this might be considered a characteristically Socialist policy. Faced with the challenge of the measures of state control introduced by the Attlee government the Conservatives produced their *Industrial Charter* in 1947, and since then Conservative governments have exercised considerable guidance over the economy. This policy was given a particular boost by Macmillan, who set up, for example, the National Economic Development Council. A traditional Conservative unlike a traditional Liberal has no inhibitions about strong government, so long as he is at the helm.

Politics is a necessary chore for the natural leaders to undertake — it is not an activity that the bulk of people need bother themselves about very much. The very function of politics is indeed thought of as providing the conditions in which people can undertake more worthwhile pursuits. Politics must be subordinate and serve these other activities. Conservatism therefore has a natural attraction for the non-political man (or woman) who prefers to cultivate his own garden. "To the great majority of Conservatives," states Lord Hailsham, "religion, art, study, family, country, friends, music, fun, duty, all the joy and riches of existence of which the poor no less than the rich are the indefeasible freeholders, all these are higher in the scale than their handmaiden, the political struggle." He evidently feels strongly about this, for he adds, "The man who puts politics first is not fit to be called a civilised being." [30]

This list of worthwhile human activities is both attractive and quite comprehensive. But, because he is an old Tory, not a new Liberal Conservative, he omits one of the most obvious features of non-political Conservatism, borrowed from laissez-faire Liberalism, namely the acquisition of wealth. One of the main purposes of Conservative government is to encourage incentive, profit and acquisition of property. People must have the incentive to work hard. Competition is therefore good and it follows that variety is necessary to provide the context for competition — whether in industry or education. There is a constant attempt by Conservative governments to reduce taxation as a fillip to individual effort — to provide the incentive of being able to enjoy the fruits of one's labour instead of having them reft from one's hand by a grasping Chancellor of the Exchequer. Free enterprise and the profit motive are economic principles dear to the Conservative, providing a system within which incentive can have free play. In practice, of course, both Labour and Conservative parties accept a mixed economy; but they have approached this position from opposite directions. The Conservative home base is free enterprise and competition. The Conservative economic ethic is indeed institutionalised in the affluent society, in which private wealth is given a higher priority than the state provision of social services. The contrast was especially noticeable in the 1950s when private material enrichment developed at a particularly fast pace. Yet, "alongside this was the evident belief of the Government that the country could not *afford* to build a single new hospital — or prison: none were built during the decade". [31]

The acquisition of wealth, however, is not seen as an end in itself, but rather as a means towards the acquisition of property — by Lockean tradition a natural right. And just as the 1950s was the period of "you've never had it so good" (Macmillan) and of "private affluence, public squalor" (Galbraith), so it was the era of the Conservative ideal of a "property-owning democracy". This was a phrase popularised by Eden, though it can already be found in the 1950 manifesto. Every family should, as far as possible, own the roof over its head.

Is Conservatism an ideology?

The man of [Conservative] disposition understands it to be the business of a government not to inflame passion and give it new objects to feed upon, but to inject into the activities of already too passionate men an ingredient of moderation ... not because passion is vice and moderation virtue, but because moderation is indispensable if passionate men are to escape being locked in an encounter of mutual frustration. [32]

Thus does Michael Oakeshott recommend Conservatism. Moreover, the Conservative believes this passion and frustration to arise from commitment to general theory and government by detailed programme. The Conservative is concerned to foster the good life and believes that this cannot result from a formula. Indeed, a coherent theory would almost be a contradiction of what Conservatism stands for — namely, the preservation of the status quo: "The ideal is broadly the real," writes Nigel Harris, "and therefore there is no need for separate ideals which contrast with reality and oblige one to change reality." [33] Suspicious of doctrine, the Conservative is rarely doctrinaire. The history of Conservatism, certainly since 1945 and in some measure since the era of Neville Chamberlain, has been a story of adaptation and accommodation to the Labour Party's principles of a managed economy and welfare state legislation (though a tradition of social reform had already been established by Disraeli and Cross in the 1870s, it is true).

However, the rejection of a major role for political theory is itself, if not an ideology, at least a belief, an attitude of mind. And even if the Conservative Party is reluctant to commit itself to a tightly-knit programme, we have already managed to indicate particular principles for which it stands and which provide a set of distinguishing features. It may be argued, of course, that these principles are couched in very general terms — hierarchy, stability, tradition — with no attempt to mould society into any set pattern. And yet a leading Conservative politician like Lord Hailsham can be pretty specific, and Conservative manifestos are clearly different from the Labour Party's.

Yet compared with Socialism, even in its present attenuated form in Britain, Conservatism is a less ideological movement in the sense of having a less comprehensive and consistent set of doctrines. Most commentators are agreed on this. It is an ethos, an attitude of mind, a mode of feeling, a disposition of mind. Such are the phrases that spring to the pen. In the final analysis, however, we must not be deceived into thinking that individual Conservatives in certain circumstances will not cling as obstinately to their principles as members of a party with a more specifically defined set of ideas. (One must, naturally, read "obstinate" as being interchangeable with "highly principled" according to taste.) Party politics in Britain has not yet been entirely reduced to vote-catching.

Liberalism

Liberalism, with a small "l", means freedom from oppression. It is a crusade fought against many infidels on behalf of individuals and large communities against economic controls and political repression. The liberal spirit was given a significant boost in the struggles against political autocracy and religious intolerance in seventeenth-century England and eighteenth-century France, while in North America it has been a constant strain throughout history from colonial days to the present. In Europe in the nineteenth century it became identified with movements of national liberation and after the First World War with the democratic reaction against monarchical autocracy. Complacent historians of the 1900s could look back over a period of steady progress as liberating reason triumphed over the dark forces of obscurantism and oppression.

In England these principles became personified in the Liberal Party in the half-century before the First World War. Feeding on the economic principles of the Manchester School and the political principles of John Stuart Mill and led by the moral dynamism of Gladstone, Liberalism became the major political force in late Victorian and Edwardian England. But as an organised political power, the Liberal Party's hour was a short one: by the 1920s it had been split asunder by the quarrel between Asquith and Lloyd George, and been overtaken on the left by the Labour Party. Support steadily declined as the party ceased to be a viable party of government. Even so, Liberalism cannot be written off as something dead and past. Many of its principles are still relevant, attractive and influential and must therefore be examined here. Contemporary Liberalism may be analysed under four headings: freedom and rights of the individual; social reform; constitutional reform; and supranationalism.

Freedom is the quintessence of liberalism. According to the constitution of the party, "in everything it puts freedom first". [34] This element in the doctrine can be traced back to the laissez-faire principles of the nineteenth century — the Cobden-Asquith branch of the family tree, based on the belief that state interference in private, especially economic, matters was not only bad in principle but also not very conducive to efficiency. Adam Smith in the eighteenth century propounded the belief in free trade, John Stuart Mill in the nineteenth, the idea of the freedom of the individual. For the Liberal it is the individual who counts, not society at large or a segment of it, for only by placing priority on the rights of the individual can freedom be ensured. Hence the modern Liberal Party's emphasis on equality of opportunity, the need for caution in state planning, humane treatment of immigrants and support for movements of national independence. However, in the twentieth century the Liberal does not advocate unbridled laissez-faire. Concern for the dignity of the individual has led the Liberal to an advocacy of social reform. This is the second branch of Liberalism, represented by the radical reformism of Joseph Chamberlain, Lloyd George and Jo Grimond. Although the Labour government of 1945-51 established the modern welfare state, it must not be forgotten that the elementary foundations had already been laid by the Liberal reforms immediately preceding 1914 and that it was the Liberal Sir William Beveridge who produced in 1942 the *Report on Social Insurance and Allied Services* that provided the framework for the post-1945 legislation. "The Liberal Party exists to build a Liberal Commonwealth in which every citizen shall possess liberty, property and security and none shall be enslaved by poverty, ignorance or unemployment." [35]

But freedom is not just freedom from want. The individual must be able to exercise effective political influence through properly constructed constitutional machinery. "Bring new life to neglected regions", "Modernise the machinery of government", demanded the Liberal manifesto in 1966. Liberals diagnose the decline of the regions outside the south-east and the decline of Parliament as serious contemporary ills. They therefore advocate constitutional reform that would involve a devolution of power to give effective power to regional councils and an electoral system that would produce a parliament more accurately reflecting the popular will. "The changes we propose would ensure that every vote cast really counted and would dispel the present electoral apathy." [36] Is it too cynical to notice that the Liberal Party has its traditional home in the underdeveloped regions of the Celtic fringe and that an electoral system in which the number of seats are more nearly proportional to the number of votes cast nationally would benefit the Liberal Party more than any other? Or is there a genuine and valuable message in the emphasis on "community" and the rejection of the monolithic nature of the two parties? Taken to its logical conclusion, this emphasis on "community" leads to a third branch of Liberalism, distinct from both the old laissez-faire and the later radicalism. It is the New Liberalism evolved by Peter Hain's Young Liberals, verging on to the communalism of the anarchists.

The Liberal wishes to see an erosion of state power. This may be achieved on the one hand by provincial devolution and on the other by the strengthening of supranational institutions.* It is consistent of the Liberals therefore to have campaigned for the strengthening of the United Nations Organisation and for Britain's admission to the Common Market. Britain must sacrifice "the growing myth of national sovereignty". [37] It is a policy, too, that is consistent with the liberal's traditional abhorrence of violence. There is a high moral tone about Liberalism, epitomised by Gladstone's thundering against the Armenian massacres and his evening ventures to rescue prostitutes from their sinful ways. "... we insist on the necessity of idealism," declared a Liberal study group in 1969, "the Conservatives have always been sceptical of idealism. This characteristic is not likely to change. But in Britain the exhaustion of the Labour Party's idealistic impulse has now created a void in political life. It is this which Liberals must fill." [38] But is their idealism divorced from realism? Does the Liberal wish "to enjoy all the fruits of politics without paying the price or noticing the pain"? [39] Is Liberalism too individualistic for the complex society of the twentieth century? Is it too undoctrinaire in an age that requires planning? Has Liberalism declined because liberalism is obsolete? Perhaps. But there is an alternative view, namely, that the principles of liberalism have been so undogmatic and so generally acceptable that, like the economic teaching of the Liberal John Maynard Keynes, they have become diffused throughout British society, adopted by all parties and therefore not needing a separate party to propagate them. In the words of two students of British Liberalism, "There is not a single institution in the country which has not felt the impact of these ideas while at the deeper level of instinctive feeling they have become a part of the national character, finding expression in the tradition of 'fair play'." [40]

---

* For a discussion of these ideas in a broader context, see below, pp. 95-102.

And in the last analysis is it not the Liberal (or liberal) tradition in British politics that is its most characteristic quality? Undoctrinaire, tolerant, jealous of the rights of the individual. It is precisely this quality that has provided its resilience and flexibility — perhaps the most precious political quality there is, enabling change to be brought about without crisis.

3 Ideological Panaceas

What is ideology?

Man is endowed by nature with the precious capacity for thought, and however materialistic we may be in our ways of life, either by choice or force of circumstance, we cannot help but formulate ideas, attitudes and beliefs about the society in which we live. For the great bulk of mankind these thoughts are crude, perhaps barely consciously held. For many, a patchwork of untidy ideas cobbled together in the mind because no single set of doctrines seems to provide a completely satisfying explanation of social relationships or guide to action: such are the moderate, pragmatic programmes of the main British political parties we have just reviewed. Others enjoy the comfortable certainty of a tightly-knit ideology — an *idée fixe* about the way to political salvation.

Ideologies have been conveniently defined as

> ... articulated sets of ideals, ends, and purposes, which help members of the system to interpret the past, explain the present, and offer a vision for the future. Thereby they describe the aims for which some members feel political power ought to be used and its limits. They may be deceptive myths about political life; they may be realistic appraisals and sincere aspirations. But they have the potential, because they are articulated as a set of ethically infused ideals, to capture the imagination.[1]

But although "ideology" is a more specific term than "ideas", it has in practice been employed with different emphases. It is the pattern of ideas thrown up automatically by specific social circumstances: all societies generate their own ideologies; it is a total, all-embracing and systematic explanatory system and plan of political action; it is a set of ideas formulated into a precise political programme; it is a fervently held but impractical formula for a political utopia. All these shades of meaning will be illustrated in the following pages.

The divisions between the next three chapters are somewhat arbitrary. All the doctrines dealt with are in effect ideologies, and the fact that there are close interrelationships between them is clear from the need to indulge in frequent cross-references. Collected into the present chapter are those ideologies which can be most clearly described as panaceas – whose exponents believe that they possess the magic key to political harmony.

Communism: the framework

In 1848 Europe was in turmoil. Almost every major city – Paris, Vienna, Berlin, Prague, Rome, Venice – seethed in revolution. Although little of permanence was achieved at the time, two German thinkers, Marx and Engels, published a pamphlet in February of that year, their manifesto which we can now see was to serve as the prologue to the modern Communist movement. In essence, Marx believed that the broad shape of historical events is determined by the economic structure of a society, which itself evolves by a process of tension between conflicting classes until history itself comes to rest, after the victory of the proletariat and the withering away of the exploitative capitalist state, in the peaceful haven of the classless, stateless Communist society. Marx conceived the final struggle – the overthrow of industrial capitalism – as an international movement, which, although starting initially and spontaneously in the most industrially developed states, would spill over any national frontiers ("Working men of all countries, unite!") and eventually engulf the whole world. Capitalism would, Marx thought, be torn apart by its own contradiction of increasing national wealth amid increasing poverty and misery for the masses. The crying injustices of industrialised societies in the mid-nineteenth century rendered Marx's analysis and forecasts very plausible. The gulf between bourgeoisie and workers was widening, the capitalist system was becoming increasingly ingrown and the workers increasingly discontented.

Marx's genius lay in his skill in knitting together into a compelling, coherent pattern a complex range of ideas and observations, and even more of teaching the inextricable interconnection between ideas and practice. From the Enlightenment he took the belief in the possibility of human progress and additionally that this progress could be most effectively achieved by the understanding and manipulation of the scientific laws that underlie human social relationships: his claim was to be the Newton of the social sciences. From Hegelian philosophy he adapted the idea of the dialectic − of change brought about by the progressive clash and fusion of mutually antithetical forces. From the events of the French Revolution he learned of the power of popular insurrection. From the early French Socialist thinkers like Saint-Simon and Proudhon he acquired the conviction of the need for a more equitable ordering of society. From the teachings of the English classical economists like Ricardo and Mill he came to appreciate the significance of economic factors in shaping our lives. From his own researches he came to believe that capitalism contained within itself the seeds of its own destruction.

We are not here primarily concerned with classical Marxism, but rather with its adjustment to present-day conditions − and his fundamental ideas do still receive a sympathetic hearing in many places where poverty and social injustice exist. Since Marx wrote, two major developments have supervened to spoil his neat programme of the destruction of the bourgeois state by a desperate proletarian uprising: living standards for the workers in industrial countries have risen, not declined; and the Communist revolution first broke out in a comparatively backward country and one which, moreover, remained the sole beneficiary of Marxist revolution for a generation. These factors have inevitably coloured assessments of the basic Marxist gospel.

Since the end of the Second World War, it is true, a number of Communist regimes have been established, almost all in eastern Europe and Asia. All but Angola, Yugoslavia, China,.Indo-china and Cuba were imposed by force of Russian arms, not by popular revolution. One of the major features of Communism since 1917, indeed, has been the tutelary control exercised by the Soviet Union, both in terms of ideological orthodoxy and its practical application. However, this authority has been steadily eroded by a number of events. Firstly, liberalising and nationalistic movements have challenged the Soviet position in eastern Europe on a number of occasions, notably in Yugoslavia, Poland, Hungary and Czechoslovakia. Secondly, Khrushchev's denunciation of Stalin in 1956 tore away the pretence of his, and hence of Moscow's, doctrinal infallibility. And thirdly, Peking has emerged as an alternative Mecca for the faithful − and a more relevant practitioner of the art of Marxist revolution for the peoples of the underdeveloped countries than the now highly industrialised Soviet Union. For in Latin America and south-east Asia particularly many seek material improvement through revolution; while, paradoxically, in the most advanced capitalist countries on both sides of the North Atlantic Ocean, Marxism has its weakest appeal. Paradoxically, too, the expansion of Communist revolution has occurred at a time of very modest contributions to Marxist theory. In the words of Isaac Deutscher,

> This is a time of triumph for Marxism only in so far as this is an age of revolution which develops an anticapitalist, a postcapitalist kind of society. But it is also an age of degeneration of Marxist thought and of intellectual decline for the labor movement at large.... We have an expansion in Marxist practice and a shrinkage and degeneration in Marxist thinking. [2]

The ideas of Karl Marx alone are complex and subtle enough; yet this basic creed has been contorted by a formidable band of interpreters, revisionists and updaters into a confusing kaleidoscope of doctrines. To change the image: Leninism has been laid on top of Marxism, and Trotskyism, Stalinism, Khrushchevism and Maoism on top of Leninism like geological layers of ideological rock. No attempt can be made here to investigate all these intricacies. It is proposed, therefore, to take four of the major facets that characterise this corpus of doctrine and to show how they have been reshaped and polished over the past generation.

The Communist theory of class conflict

> The history of all hitherto existing society is the history of class struggle.... Our epoch, the epoch of the bourgeoisie, possesses, however, this distinctive feature: It has simplified the class antagonisms. Society as a whole is more and more splitting up into two great hostile camps, into two great classes directly facing each other — bourgeoisie and proletariat. [3]

For Marx, as for all his subsequent adherents, the division of society into discrete, antagonistic classes, and in particular the current irreconcilable enmity between the capitalist and working classes is the bedrock of Communist theory and social analysis.

How does the Marxist perceive these opposing classes? Firstly, the bourgeoisie: these are the owners of businesses and factories, financiers and rentiers — a sizeable group, though the numbers of actual property owners decline with the concentration of wealth that is the mark of capitalist development. They own the means of production, distribution and exchange. More than that, they have consolidated their economic power by building up monopolies, extended it by the trading and investment opportunities provided by imperialism and have seized and consolidated power in the political field as the state has been drawn into supporting the capitalist system. On the other hand, although the bourgeois *enjoy* wealth, it is the labour of the working classes that in reality *produces* it; yet the workers remain to all intents and purposes propertyless. Vis-à-vis the bourgeoisie the workers are clearly in a weak position. Thus both at the national and the international level members of the working class are constantly being exhorted by the Communists to band together, to exploit their only strength, namely, their numbers. The need for class solidarity was even used by Khrushchev in his denunciation of Yugoslav neutrality in the Cold War, which, he declared, weakened "the forces of the revolutionary movement, the forces of Socialism, and [aided] the enemies of the working class". [4] It is a message constantly reiterated in *The British Road to Socialism,* the official programme of the British Communist Party. [5] This document also shows how Communists are at pains to demonstrate that the maintenance of the status quo is by no means in the workers' interests:

> The Communist Party believes that if our people are to enjoy a life of opportunity and prosperity and Britain play a progressive role in the world a new social system is needed, for the present one is increasingly failing. The working people will have to make a revolutionary change, end capitalism and build a socialist society. Only then, when the people own the means of production and decide their own destiny, will the miracles of modern science perform miracles for the welfare of the great majority. [6]

Although the working class in capitalist countries are exhorted to struggle to unseat the bourgeoisie from their favoured positions, the collapse of capitalism is believed in the long run to be inevitable: inevitable in theory because of the inexorability of the historical forces at work; inevitable in practice because of the inner contradiction from which the capitalist system suffers. Marx emphasised that capitalism is based on a fundamental anomaly that would eventually sunder the whole structure. This anomaly (or contradiction as Marx called it) is the combination of private ownership and profit-seeking with the socially interconnected network of its mode of operation. Revolution in the industrially advanced Western states seems further away than in 1848; but the morale of the faithful is sustained by the belief — the knowledge rather — that the bourgeois system must snap under the tension of this contradiction. And it is the messianic function of the working class to assume control, first of all in the transitionary phase of the dictatorship of the proletariat (the stage reached by the so-called Communist states today) as a preparation for the true Communist utopia which will then follow.

Since 1945 class conflict, it may be argued, has manifested itself in three major forms. In the countries of Western Europe, especially Britain, France and Italy, Communists have secured influential positions in trade unions, whence they have on occasion launched body-punches at the economies of these capitalist states by the fermentation of strikes in vitally important industries. Secondly, of course, people's democracies and republics have been set up in certain countries of eastern Europe and Asia, marking victories of the working classes. Finally, the class war can be represented as being played out on the broader, global stage, the Communist states acting out the role of the working class and the capitalist countries, the bourgeoisie. For a generation following the October Revolution Russia lay surrounded by hostile capitalist states, the embattled citadel of Socialism. To loyal Communists the fortunes of the world's workers were dependent upon the strength of the Soviet Union. Parties throughout the world looked to Moscow for support, and Moscow in its turn expected loyalty, even obedience from the "fraternal parties". Communism and Sovietism were synonymous; and the continuing influence of the Soviet Union to this day over the policies pursued by the people's democracies of Eastern Europe is a remnant of this version of international working-class solidarity.

Is class conflict the truly pivotal feature of human relationships that Marxists believe? Such social divisions do indeed generate bitter hatred. However, the doctrine presupposes a rigid demarcation unsoftened by the social mobility or charitable legislation which in practice the advanced industrialised countries have enjoyed. And more than one commentator has noted that sustained, even strengthened governmental machinery in the Communist states has coincided with the cry of capitalist encirclement or counter-revolution. Hypocrisy, convenience or chance? Whatever the explanation, the destruction of the bourgeoisie in the Communist countries has been rapidly followed by the elevation of Party members to privileged professional positions and enhanced standards of living — the establishment, in fact, of a New Class.*

The Party

A man may protest that he is not superstitious but still cross his fingers when walking under a ladder, "just in case". So Marxists insist on the inevitability of the collapse of capitalism, but urge on the workers to action, just in case. History needs a helping hand. And similarly the workers are assisted in their historical role by the leadership of the Party. Well before the 1917 Revolution Lenin preached the supreme importance of the Party, challenging the advocates of spontaneity. In 1920 he succinctly explained his position: "The Communist Party is the organised political lever by means of which the more advanced part of the working class leads all the proletarian and semi-proletarian mass in the right direction." [7] Moreover, this theoretical viewpoint has since been frequently vindicated in practice, for as the programme of the British Communist Party points out: "Socialism has never been won in any country except under the democratic, disciplined, organised leadership of parties with a clear aim and a clear understanding of the means to attain it." [8] (That may, of course, just be another way of saying that in Communist countries Socialism has been forced on an unwilling majority by a powerful minority.)

The Party, then, is not primarily designed as a mass movement, but as an élite to mobilise and direct the mass movement. Only by establishing this point can a whole range of characteristics and events be understood. Although there are plenty of self-seekers, as in all organisations, Communist Parties contain more than their fair share of dedicated workers, striving for the cause, contributing personal views but unquestioningly accepting discipline through the accepted system of "democratic centralism". The true Party member is one whose whole life is moulded by the Party — inevitably, since it is the embodiment of an all-embracing philosophy. In the words of Arthur Koestler: "My

* This is the title of a book by the Yugoslav Milovan Djilas. He was imprisoned for daring to denounce the phenomenon in print — a very good reason for accepting the validity of the thesis.

Party education had equipped my mind with such elaborate shock-absorbing buffers and elastic defences that everything seen or heard became automatically transformed to fit the preconceived pattern." [9] By establishing such a tightly-knit organisation the Party is able to wield far greater influence than conventional party machines — to achieve more with less support. However, efficiency and drive can be sustained only by sustaining standards of ardour and through a constant sifting of Party membership. This sifting process may be either voluntary or enforced. There is the self-regulating device of resignation by the disillusioned, well documented in a host of autobiographical studies like *The God That Failed*, and dramatised at such times of crisis as the withdrawal of over a fifth of the membership of the British Party when the Soviet Union suppressed the Hungarian uprising in 1956. More sensational, of course, are the violent purges such as occurred in Russia in 1936-38 and which explain, at least in some measure, the excesses of the Cultural Revolution in China. For the Party must be kept not only pure in mind but loyal and subordinate to the leader.

Stalin's ruthless treatment of the CPSU led to a reaction against the cult of personality after his death in 1953. Three years later, Khrushchev, egged on by the Party oligarchs, made his famous speech of denunciation at the Twentieth Congress. Significantly, the tenor of the speech was an attack on Stalin, as oppressor of the Party, not as oppressor of the people.

The activities and policies of the major Communist Parties outside the USSR were controlled from 1947 to 1956 by the operations of the Cominform in Moscow. The British Communist Party was not one of these. Indeed, the British Party has never been particularly significant. Founded in the aftermath of the Bolshevik Revolution and reaching the peak of its popularity with a membership of 65,000 at the time of Stalingrad, its fortunes often seemed closely tied with those of the USSR. But in the mid-1950s many became disenchanted with what the Soviet regime stood for and how the British Party was managed, at a time when Britain had never had it so good and revolutionary ardour was cooled by the pleasant breeze of economic prosperity. So that now it can be said that "British Communists do not seem to have much in common with the Russian élite. . . . They are not power-orientated tacticians. . . . In the past twenty years or so they have come to accept the principles of British parliamentary democracy." [10] Scarcely the militant vanguard of the red revolution envisaged by Lenin.

The Red Revolution

The consummation of Communist activity is the violent overthrow of the capitalist system. This is "the revolution" for which the Party cadres in capitalist states prepare and strive. It is clear that Marx's early writings and Lenin's throughout envisaged the destruction of bourgeois society by movements of popular insurrection. The *Manifesto,* for example, is quite unequivocal:

> The Communists disdain to conceal their views and aims. They openly declare that their ends can be attained only by the forcible overthrow of all existing social conditions. Let the ruling classes tremble at a communist revolution. The proletarians have nothing to lose but their chains. They have a world to win. [11]

And yet we can read the following statement in *The British Road to Socialism:* "It is in the best interests of the working people, of the vast majority of the nation, that this mass struggle for political power should be carried through by peaceful means, without civil war." [12] It is necessary to ask, therefore, precisely what is the role of revolution (as traditionally understood, namely a violent overthrow of government and social system) in Communist theory and practice.

One could make a striking juxtaposition of contrasts: the theory presupposes urban insurrection by an industrial proletariat whereas in practice most Communist regimes have been established by the force of highly organised armies and most insurrections since 1949 have been peasant-based. Unfortunately, this neat antithesis will not do justice to the complexity of the situation. The Russian Revolution adhered reasonably closely to the classical pattern; the Chinese Revolution, whatever its form, clearly enjoyed widespread support; and, in any case, theory has been constantly adjusted to take account of situations not foreseen by Marx in 1848. The most important adaptation of theory has been the growing recognition of the revolutionary potential of the peasantry. Marx thought them a conservative force; Lenin appreciated the need for their support; while the modern revolutionaries, starting with Mao and continuing with the Latin-American based Castro, Guevara and Debray, utterly reverse Marx's position and place their total faith in a revolutionary peasantry. The germ of revolution is now to be cultivated in the peasant "foco" in the forests of Latin America rather than the party "cell" in a European factory; and guerrilla tactics are now preferred to barricades.

However, not all revolutions, by Marxist definition, lead to the creation of a Communist society. Revolutions come, rather, in two forms: bourgeois-democratic and socialist. Using this terminology, the February Revolution in Russia in 1917 was bourgeois-democratic; the October Revolution, socialist. The bourgeois revolution must normally precede the socialist revolution which heralds the coming of Communism. In Russia the two events happened in rapid succession; in England the winning of parliamentary control over the Stuart monarchy in the seventeenth century was the bourgeois revolution — the socialist revolution is still awaited. That a bourgeois revolution is necessary to overthrow feudalism and a socialist revolution needed to overturn capitalism is a fundamental tenet of Marx's philosophy of the dialectical progression of the historical process. It would be scarcely possible to reject this idea and remain a Marxist. Mao has just kept within the rules by propounding his theory of the new democratic revolution in which both processes occur simultaneously, bourgeoisie, proletariat and peasantry joining forces to overthrow the hated *ancien regime.* However, even when the socialist revolution has been accomplished, this is not the moment for the victorious workers to rest on their laurels — at least, not in the view of Trotsky and other exponents of the "permanent revolution": the victory must be consolidated by reforms and spread to other lands. Trotsky summed up the theory of the permanent revolution in a book of that title:

> The conquest of power by the proletariat does not terminate the revolution, but only opens it. Socialist construction is conceivable only on the foundation of the class struggle, on a national and international scale. This struggle, under the conditions of an overwhelming predominance of capitalist relationships in the world arena, will inevitably lead to explosions, that is internally to civil wars and externally to revolutionary wars. Therein lies the permanent character of the socialist revolution as such. [13]

The essence of revolution is a transfer of political and economic power. Is violence also necessary? Both on a national and an international level there is considerable support in Marxist literature for the view that it is: the bourgeoisie will fight to retain their possessions. Castro put it quite bluntly: "To us the international communist movement is in the first place just that, a movement of communists, of revolutionary fighters. And those who are not revolutionary fighters cannot be called communists." [14]   On an international scale the revolution means a struggle between capitalist and Communist states; and if violence is necessary at this level, this means war — even in the age of thermonuclear weapons. It is to this strict, Leninist interpretation of the international scene that Mao tenaciously holds, denouncing as reformist revisionists those Marxists who believe that revolution can be achieved without resort to violence.

Social reform

The aim of Communism is the amelioration of the lot of the working class. All Communists accept this, but they are utterly split on the issue of whether violent revolution is a necessary precondition. If violence is not assumed to be necessary, a whole range of techniques for effecting reform are opened up. If Communists so wish they can operate through the institutions that exist in many capitalist countries, namely parliament and trade unions. Depending on their electoral strength, they may be a parliamentary force in their own right, or, alternatively, may seek to collaborate with other left-wing groups. Chile provided an excellent example of the way Communists can achieve power by the ordinary processes of democratic parliamentary elections when, in 1970, the Marxist Dr Salvador Allende won the presidency at the head of the Popular Unity Alliance. Alternatively, the trade unions may be used as pressure groups to achieve better working conditions and wages. Members of the British Communist Party, for example, exercise a disproportionate influence compared with their numbers in industries like the docks and engineering because of their drive and organising skill. On an international level, too, violence has been renounced by a number of parties in the belief that more can be done for the cause and in practical terms for ordinary people by economic rather than military competition with capitalist states.

In many ways the 1950s proved a turning point. The Italian Party leader, Togliatti, was pleading for a less dogmatic line on the transition to Communism — each country, he argued, should pursue the path that most suited its traditions and needs. In 1956 this idea was accorded Khrushchev's seal of approval in a speech which was given less publicity in the West than his attack on Stalin, but which doctrinally was more important. The dictatorial Stalinist control of all other Parties, and the stern Leninist acceptance of the need to resort to violence, were to be thrown to the winds and the creeds of the different roads to Socialism and peaceful coexistence set in their place. But the Hungarian uprising that followed discredited the new line. The Chinese vigorously denounced what they considered to be a betrayal of established Leninist doctrine and the quarrel deteriorated yearly until even fighting broke out between the two countries on the Manchurian frontier. In the 1970s a softer "Eurocommunism" developed in Western Europe.

One of the many attractions in replacing revolution by reform lay in the expected relaxation of government and Party control: a relaxation, indeed, of the siege mentality. In 1968 the Czechs followed through this position to its logical conclusion. Under the leadership of Alexander Dubček a whole series of reforms was planned, both economic and political, in order to provide "socialism with a human face". An Action Programme was devised which recognised that the "social revolution" had entered a new "epoch of non-antagonistic relations" and that consequently there was a "need to develop, shape and create a political system that would correspond to the new situation". "The party decisively condemn", the programme roundly proclaimed, "the attempts to set individual classes and groups of socialist society against each other, and it will remove every cause creating tensions among them." [15] The Soviet leaders, however, considered the Czechs dangerously adventuresome and crushed the Dubček regime by a military invasion. Luckily for the British Communist Party their reformist policies are not perceived as a threat to Moscow. Lenin urged that the Communist Party of Great Britain should support the Labour Party "as the rope supports a hanging man". [16] Nevertheless, the current programme foresees a more collaborative relationship, a closer drawing together with the left-wing element in the Labour Party, which is firmly rejected by some unofficial elements in the trade unions. [17] The Party seeks, indeed, "new political alignments" which would "create the conditions for the election of a Parliamentary majority and government pledged to a socialist programme". [18] The whole emphasis is on legislative reform within the established system: the word "revolution" hardly appears in the document at all.

The condition of Communism today
We live in a world where the inefficiencies and abuses of the capitalist system are plain to see and where the gap between the rich and poor countries yawns ever wider. Does Communism provide an attractive answer to these problems? The question can be subdivided into three

components: how valid and attractive are the philosophical bases of Marxism, the four live issues of the system identified above, and the society that is the end-product of the Marxist process?

Despite all his qualifications, Marx painted a picture of the broad development of human society as predetermined by economic forces. Much occurs that is indeed beyond the individual's control and Marx has put every historian, social scientist and politician in his debt by emphasising the very powerful influence that economic forces exercise over our lives. And yet there comes a sticking point beyond which many people refuse to go. Man is surely not motivated solely by economic pressures? Is religion, are the arts, really reducible ultimately to economic explanations? And is mankind really so powerless to shape his own destiny? Can he really do no more than hasten or retard processes which are in essence inevitable? Newton dazzled the eighteenth-century mind by reducing the wanderings of the planets to the most simple mathematical explanations. Marx sought to achieve similar scientific laws to explain the behaviour of societies. The reduction of human behaviour to such a mechanistic level is not a very attractive thesis.

A similar admiration for his perceptiveness accompanied by a reluctance to accept his analysis as the total truth may also be the experience derived from examining some of the more detailed features of Marx's system. Class divisions have become fudged rather than polarised with increasing social mobility and diffusion of wealth; the Party has failed to win over the mass of the proletariat, who look for salvation rather to programmes of social democracy; while revolution is not an attractive prospect against the firmly entrenched modern state.

And what of the Communist goal? Here we must distinguish carefully between practice and theory. In practice Communist regimes are marked by an offensively authoritarian style of government — to the point of totalitarianism at times. It is a moot point, of course, whether this authoritarianism is intrinsic to Marxism or the result of the particular circumstances in which Communism has developed. Communist regimes are, in practice, characterised by a planned economy, powerful bureaucracy and a one-party political system. Defendants of the ideology argue that these features are the result of economic scarcity: developing wealth will lead to liberalisation. Increased wealth did lead to liberalisation in Czechoslovakia; but the regime was not allowed to survive. We are left with the uncertainty. On the other hand, the theory promises a classless, depoliticised society. Is this desirable, or even possible? It may be considered, after all, that the competitive spirit of human nature and the complex requirements of modern technological economy render the idea quite impractical.

Marx sought to create a science of society; he produced a secular religion. It is balm to the faithful, anathema to the followers of other creeds and of academic rather than emotional interest to the ideologically agnostic.

The New Left

For the man who harbours with some bitterness his resentment against the injustices of society and the state as they are currently organised, Communism has, for the past century, provided an intellectual refuge. However, when the Communist refuge becomes a prison as offensive as the capitalist gaol, the radical must resume his intellectual journeying. Disillusion came to many with the horrors of Stalinist totalitarianism. But no vigorous alternative was forthcoming until the 1960s. Then at last a new generation, offended by Soviet action in Hungary and Czechoslovakia and by what they interpreted as the betrayal of the revolutionary tradition by the moderate tactics of many a Communist Party, fumbled its way towards a new utopian doctrine. In 1968 they seized public attention by a series of dramatic outbursts in both the USA and Europe.

This new movement was too amorphous to be called an organisation — indeed, there is a considerable ingredient of anarchist individualism in the mixture. (The most extremist groups are the anarchists, but since they have a distinct view about the use of political power they will be discussed separately in Chapter 4.) Clusters of small groups, usually youthful in age, but often led by ex-Communists, sometimes quarrelling with each other, but sharing a common hatred of modern, industrial society emerged especially in the Western hemisphere. Their alienation from the regimentation of industrial society led this New Left to recognise its intellectual roots in the early writings of Marx where he emphasised this social problem of alienation — roots which, it so happens, were already being nurtured by scholars like Adorno and Marcuse of the Frankfurt School of Sociology. The theory of alienation holds that capitalism has divorced us all in our work from any meaningful perception of its product, even of man's very place in nature.

Exponents of the ideology of the New Left may be broadly classified into five groups according to the particular ideas they emphasise, which in turn have been dependent on the circumstances in which the groups have originated and worked. First, the Anarchists. Secondly, there are the Trotskyists, supporters of a revolutionary tradition founded by Stalin's most distinguished opponent. They retain a strongly anti-Soviet stance, believing that the revolution there has been utterly distorted by nationalist and bureaucratic considerations and that the true Marxist revolution which they — largely trade unionists and students — must work for must be international and must be led from below, not by an élite of party bureaucrats. In Britain, Trotskyism was kept before the public eye by the remarkable success of the newspaper *The Red Mole*, organ of the faction known as the International Marxist Group. The other political giant in the Marxist revolutionary tradition who has generated splinter groups of enthusiastic supporters was Mao Tse-tung. Inspiration for these groups derives from the immortal *Thoughts* of the Chinese leader and from his practical achievements in creating a society which appears to accord top priority to the interests of the working class and gives due recognition to honest toil. The creed has achieved most success in the West among the factory-workers of France where it has caused considerable embarrassment to the official Communist Party. The Maoists were perhaps the most intensely earnest of the New Left, pondering as they do on such puritanical thoughts as, "A good comrade is more eager to go where the difficulties are greater." [19]

Trotsky and Mao belong to historical events and movements which have a significance in their own right. But the New Left movement has thrown up its own personalities — a cluster of brilliant young men of both intellectual power and practical revolutionary experience, who have become cult figures especially among students. "Che lives"; and so does Fanon. Guevara struggled for the Latin American peon, Fanon for the African peasant, Cleaver for the American ghetto Negro, but in reality their messages were universal, directed to the oppressed wherever they might live. Guevara caught the imagination of youth more remarkably than any other; nor are the explanations difficult to come by. He was young (only thirty-nine when he died), handsome, courageous to the point of martyrdom for his cause, incredibly versatile; doctor and diplomat, financier and guerrilla leader; and, above all, he consciously rejected the comfortable life that was his for the asking to devote himself to his cause. Yet Fanon's work is of deeper significance. Drawing on his knowledge of psychiatry and his painful experiences in the Algerian war, he developed the notion of a world-wide, colonised proletariat damned to a wretched existence and identified, usually, by their coloured skins. Salvation, he argued, lies in revolution: not a mealy-mouthed changeover of politicians, but the seizure and retention of power by "the damned"*, galvanised into activity by the cleansing force of violence which "frees the native from his inferiority complex and from his despair and inaction". [20]

There is visionary romanticism in Guevara, fierce fanaticism in Fanon. The philosophising, the intellectual appeal to the students of the University of California, the London School of Economics and the Sorbonne, was woven by Marcuse and Sartre. Marcuse, from his professorial chair at Berkeley, California, has constructed a view of capitalist democratic society as oppressive as fascism. Because the purblind indoctrinated masses are unconscious of their condition, tolerance is a positive danger, indeed a consciously administered opium of the masses. Tolerance must not be tolerated. The whole structure must be overthrown.

Because the New Left was so diverse in its origins and appeal it is a little difficult to generalise about the distinguishing features of its ideology. However, there are certain basic ideas that are fairly widely held across the spectrum. The starting-point is, of course, the belief in the utter degradation, corruption and oppression of virtually every established political regime, of whatever complexion. Modern society generally, it is held, is ordered for the benefit of an élite, whether this is viewed primarily in political, economic, social or racial terms. The quality of life, the dignity of the individual, a sense of true community has been sacrificed time and time again on the altars of power and prestige. This falseness of modern life is what Marx termed "alienation" and this is where the Marxist style of thinking is most clearly evident. "Men do not live their own lives," writes Marcuse, "but perform pre-established functions. While they work, they do not fulfil their own needs and faculties, but work in alienation." [21] Similarly, Guevara believed that "the ultimate goal of the Revolution was to set men free from their alienation from their society, which they miscalled their individualism. 'In spite of the apparent standardisation of man in

---

* *Les Damnés de la terre* is the title of his most famous work, usually translated as *The Wretched of the Earth*, but "wretched" is a feeble word.

socialism, he is more complete.' " [22]

How, then, are the desirable changes to be effected? Clearly the revolutionary role falls to the down-trodden. But they are a motley crew: blue-collared trade unionists, disaffected middle-class students, economically depressed American Negroes, ragged Latin-American peasants and African victims of colonialism and neo-colonialism. They all share the opportunity of becoming conscious of the oppression wrought by modern class-ridden society, of recognising that the claims of social justice are façades. It is realised, of course, that not all members of these groups by any means will achieve their potential, not all will receive the message. Fermented New Left '68 is an acquired taste; the revolution must be brought about by the outsiders with a connoiseur's palate. It might be thought difficult to fit students into this category. But they have also felt that they were facing bureaucratic anonymity in their overgrown universities. Also, association with the New Left was provided an outlet for frustrated intellectual youth. To the members of Students for a Democratic Society American society is a juggernaut that has already threatened the lives and happiness of millions of Vietnamese peasants and American Negroes and must be stopped before wreaking more havoc.

Modern states are powerful institutions. Violence is clearly necessary to achieve any effect. Since, in any case, modern society is perceived as organised violence, violence must be countered with violence. Thus the Negroes must become, in the words of Stokeley Carmichael, "the executioners of our executioners", [23] — a conscious reversal of the non-violent policy of Martin Luther King. Sartre and Marcuse, too, advocate violence. Fanon, as has already been mentioned, raised violence to a solemn rite — more: a psychological need.

There were, in fact, deep psychological undercurrents in the New Left. The psychiatrist R.D. Laing has gone so far as to declare that it is the schizophrenic who is sane; society, mad. The belief that the evils of society are the results of sexual repression has an especially wide currency among the New Left. This belief has led to a number of symbolic acts such as the innocuous occupation of women's hostels by male French students to the calculated rape of a white woman as a defiant act of insurrection by the Black Panther leader, Eldridge Cleaver. As one would expect from his training as a psychiatrist, it is Fanon of the major New Left thinkers who has written most explicitly on the subject, identifying the precise forms of white-black tension in psychosexual neurosis. This train of thought reaches its climax in the ideas of Wilhelm Reich, who provides a totally sexual explanation of politics. Oppression and repression are banished at a stroke.

The high water mark of New Left action was the May rebellion in France in 1968. Student troubles escalated until France was paralysed by strikes and the country was brought to the brink of full-scale revolution. The crisis destroyed De Gaulle's credibility as a political leader. It is instructive in a number of ways. The initiative and influence of the university students was the most notable feature. Yet, they had no effective organisation: the student protest was remarkable for its spontaneity; and the movement was as littered with confusing initials indicative of the diverse range of "groupuscules" as the Sorbonne was with rubbish indicative of the casual manner of the revolutionaries. The lack of ideological cohesion is splendidly exemplified by the fact that the most famous spokesman, Daniel Cohn-Bendit, denied membership of any of the groups — except his own Movement of 22 March! Of course, it takes more than a cluster of students to make a revolution: what rendered the situation so dangerous was the immediate support of some industrial workers and the fear that it might spread. And, most revealing of all, it is difficult to estimate who was embarrassed more by the whole situation, the French government or the Communist Party, which quickly brought its members back into line and away from the heterodox students.

Orthodox Communism and the New Left were uncomfortable bedfellows. For if there is something that a Communist really must have it is discipline and rules. His Marxism is a scientific, rational doctrine. The New Left was often irrational, violent and intolerant but it is also speculative and imaginative. The new spectre that is haunting the world is perhaps even more gruesome than the old.

Racialism
The New Left seeks salvation through a reduction in the power of the state apparatus and an enhanced social conscience. Individuals are rated for their *personal* worth. Racialism, on the other hand, emphasises the differences between *groups*, defined ethnically, and places its trust for human progress in segregation and domination.

We must, first, distinguish between the biological construct — race, and the social ideology — racialism. The concept "race" merely posits the scientific possibility and usefulness of classifying mankind into a number of distinguishable groups. Racialism — that is, making judgments about groups in terms of supposed relative human worth — need not necessarily follow from this scientific exercise. It was in the eighteenth century that biologists became obsessed with classifying and categorising every living thing they could identify. And why should man be excluded? The problem is, what variables do you use in the categorising process? One possibility is culture — the religious or artistic expressions of a people. Anti-semitism, for example, has been based essentially on the religious identification of the Jews; similarly, the idea of *négritude* is based on the common cultural heritage of the Negro. However, race is strictly a biological concept and the biologist is interested far more in the genetically inherited than the socially acquired characteristics. It is not, therefore, surprising to find these culturally defined categories reinforced by physical tests — by the Nazi policy of nose measurement and the African's pride in his blackness. Classification by physical characteristics is, of course, the essence of racial categorisation. Skin colour and distribution of body-hair are commonly used tests, though exact distinctions are difficult to draw and no biologist would be prepared to state with precision how many races mankind is divided into. Physical characteristics like skin pigmentation are obviously inherited. But what about intelligence? It is commonly argued that intelligence is the combined product of both heredity and environment. The American psychologist Jensen has recently stirred up a hornets' nest by alleging that American Negroes are genetically inferior in intelligence to American whites — that is, as a group, US Negroes would rate lower than white even if their social, economic and educational opportunities were the same. Jensen's thesis is so controversial because it contains a value judgment. To state that Negroes have black skins and Europeans have white is purely descriptive; to state that one group is more intelligent than another is to imply that one group is *better* than another.

It is precisely this kind of social judgment that transmutes race into racialism. There is nothing new about this. Under the influence of evolutionary biology the very process of classification was bound to lead, in the late eighteenth century, to the production of hierarchical patterns. If men belong to different races, it is but a short step to argue that some must be "better" than others — firstly, that some have evolved further than others; secondly, that in a Darwinian sense, some are fitter to survive than others; and thirdly, that some actually corrupt the others and must be removed, as the Nazis both preached and practised. The first belief led the President of the Anthropological Society of London in 1863 to declare that "the analogies are far greater between the Negro and the ape than between the European and the ape"; [24] while the others led inexorably to the creed of the Master Race.

Racialism is the belief that the difference between races should be recognised by social and political arrangements and in particular that racial superiority should be rewarded by social and political privilege. Like nationalism, it is a response to the very powerful human urge to achieve an identification with a cohesive group. And so, just as the nationalist searches for a *cultural* means of distinction such as language, so the racialist seeks to emphasise distinguishing *physical* features like colour.

How did the racialist idea become formulated? The foundations were laid down in the half-century or so before the First World War — by the writings of the Frenchman Count Gobineau, the German Richard Wagner and the Englishman H.S. Chamberlain: a fusion of influences from the findings of the biological revolution and the experiences of the age of imperialism. Following the attempts to categorise mankind into a hierarchy of races, defined according to characteristics like colour, these writers produced the further refinement of positing a hierarchy *within* the white race. Nineteenth-century philological research suggested that many European and Asiatic languages had a common root — this led to the hypothesis of an "Aryan" language. The racial theorists made the quite unwarranted leap of asserting that this *linguistic* group enjoyed common *physical* features. In his *Essay on the Inequality of the Human Races* Gobineau argued a correlation between the fortunes of civilisation and the division of mankind into races: civilisations decay when their populations are adulterated by the influx of new races; the Aryans, however, because of their superior endowments, were leading mankind to an unsurpassed level of civilisation. Gobineau's ideas soon gained wide currency, especially among the Germans who were thought to be the purest strain of the Aryan race. Even Gobineau societies sprang up.

Gobineau was not an obsessive ideologue and by no means preached racial persecution. But by the end of the century writers like the great German composer Wagner were using Gobineau's ideas to preach Teutonic greatness and to warn of the threat presented by the clannish

Jewish race. Wagner believed in the greatness of the German hero-spirit and came to propagate racialist theories to support this idea. But it was left to Wagner's son-in-law, Houstan Stewart Chamberlain, to pour out the racialist ideology in all its dogmatism, illogicality and inaccuracy in his popular *Foundations of the Nineteenth Century*, published in 1899. "The Teuton is the soul of our culture", he declared. And: "To this day these two powers — Jews and Teutonic races — stand, wherever the recent spread of the Chaos has not blurred its features, now as friendly, now as hostile, but always as alien forces face to face." [25] Thus, by the turn of the century the raw materials of Hitler's *Mein Kampf,* the idea of the Master Race and antisemitism, were already to hand. And the present day generalised racialist belief in the need to maintain racial distinctiveness and superiority seeped into popular consciousness.

Racialism expresses itself in four different ways. At its simplest, racialism is prejudice; put into positive operation, this becomes discrimination; the need to retain distinctive characteristics leads to segregation; the ultimate is genocide.

People are prejudiced when they express for a group a dislike unfounded on accurate factual knowledge: prejudice is irrational hostility. In itself it is merely an attitude of mind; whether it leads to racialist action is dependent on the prevailing social and political conditions and the strength with which the feeling is held. There is a well-established correlation between strong feelings of enmity and an authoritarian personality pattern, clearly revealed in Hitler's career. The classic work in this field was undertaken by Adorno and his colleagues, who declared that intense hostility to "out-groups" springs

> from underlying hostility towards in-group authorities, originally the parents. The individual strives to keep his hostility in check by over-doing in the direction of respect, obedience, gratitude towards the in-group authorities and by displacing the underlying hostility towards these authorities on to "out-groups". [26]

Prejudice may be translated into social action by the operation of discriminatory practices. And just as an individual may be mildly or pathologically prejudiced, so a society may operate discrimination in a vague and haphazard way or it may be institutionalised in quite rigid form. Most discrimination in Britain is of an unofficial kind: coloured people are denied employment or promotion of which they are worthy and they are refused accommodation that is known to be vacant, even though such practices are now technically illegal. [27] Semi-official discrimination has been practised in the USA where Negroes in the southern states have until recently been denied the right to vote not technically because of their colour but through the operation in some states of such devices as literacy tests and poll-tax qualification. Overt, officially-framed discrimination is most blatant in South Africa, of course, symbolised by the notorious pass-book system.

Discrimination involves distinctive treatment of people of different races in a mixed population. A policy of distinctive treatment may lead ultimately to the physical filtering out of the subordinate group. Thus the Jews in Warsaw congregated in their ghetto and the Negroes of New York herded into Harlem. The location of the disadvantaged racial group in the portion of an urban area that is economically and socially degraded is one of the commonest and most dispiriting aspects of inter-race relations in our day. However, only the Afrikaners in South Africa have pursued the policy to its logical end and devised a system whose ultimate goal is the complete geographical segregation of the white from the non-white races by dividing up the whole country. The aim of "A number of fully Bantu-governed states linked with the white Republic of South Africa in a co-operative association — a South African commonwealth of nations" [28] seems innocent enough. There would indeed be nothing particularly racialist about a policy that provided for genuine development of the white and non-white peoples along separate paths if they both wished it. But there is a double racialist catch: first, apartheid is not just a policy, it is an ideology fervently believed in by the Afrikaners and imposed upon the vast majority of the population who are prevented by the complex apparatus of a fully-fledged police-state from voicing their opinion; and second, "separate development" means 13 per cent of the land for 83 per cent of the population. With Calvinist religious passion, with careful Afrikaner deliberation, politicians like Malan and Verwoerd have steered the whole country since 1948 by skilfully chartered leglislation towards a rigidly structured stratified society.

Inflexible adherence to the ideology of apartheid, like the inflexible adherence to the ideology of Nazism, has led to a totalitarian exercise of power.* Mercifully, the parallel is not exact. The Nazis aimed at the utter annihilation of their subordinate racial group and in large

* See chapter 4

measure succeeded. After all, when the prime function of segregation is not socio-economic but biological, to prevent miscegenation, the only foolproof way to ensure against the danger is, like Herod faced with a different danger, to destroy all possible sources of peril.

The idea of racialism has strong and extensive roots in modern society. Not only apartheid and the Nazis' "final solution", but the activities of the Ku Klux Klan, the "White Australia" policy and "Paki-bashing" in London are all examples, at very different levels of intensity, of racialist feeling. And added to these examples, there is the general thesis that the world is divided between the rich, ex-imperialist countries and the poor, underdeveloped, coloured ex-colonies: a global racial schism. [29] How can one explain the widespread appeal of racialism? Three general factors must be taken into account, socio-economic, historical and psychological, together with the particular issue of colour.

Racial tension occurs when a subordinate race resents its comparatively lowly socio-economic status or a dominant group fears for its privileges. The angry urban riots that swept the USA in the summer months of the mid-1960s were fiery explosions of resentment against a social system in which, generally speaking, the Negro enjoys a standard of living markedly inferior to that of the white American. Racial anger is stoked by this correlation between skin colour and economic status. The situation is inverted when the out-group is, or is thought to be, economically successful. Thus the commercial expertise of Jews in Europe and Chinese in south-east Asia has bred jealousy; while prejudice in Britain often contains a large element of fear that immigrants will be given employment that might otherwise be open to white people.

A feeling as intensely held as racialism cannot develop overnight: it is the product of historical circumstances that have accustomed people to think of certain races playing accepted social roles. Racialism results from an excessive consciousness of these traditional roles. Colour consciousness is a particularly vivid example of this. As the result of European commercial and imperial expansion from c. 1500, coloured peoples were placed in conditions of inferiority vis-à-vis the white man: economically exploited, politically controlled, even sold into slavery. The inferior position of the coloured man came to be accepted as normal. This gave the white man a superiority complex, expressed sometimes brutally as in the inhumane transatlantic slave trade, sometimes paternally as in Kipling's cult of the White Man's Burden. Thus, in Britain there is an undertone of condescension in attitudes towards people whose origins may be traced back to former colonial possessions in the Caribbean or the Indian subcontinent. Historical consciousness is most painful in the USA where little over a century ago Negroes were in the veritable subhuman category of slavery. The sheer raw primitiveness of anti-black emotions in the Deep South, where lynching has been an almost accepted feature of everyday life, has few parallels in the history of racialism outside the gruesome aberration of Nazism. Much of the bitterness of modern black racialist movements in the 1960s like the Black Panthers may be attributed to the inferiority complex and the vengeful spirit these memories invoke. It has been expressed vigorously by one of the founders of the Black Panthers in the following words: "If we compromise one iota we will be selling our freedom out. We will be selling the revolution out. And we refuse to remain slaves. As Eldridge says in *Soul on Ice,* 'a slave who dies of natural causes will not balance two dead flies on the scales of eternity'."[30] Lincoln could free the United States of the institution of slavery; what he could not do was to free it of its slavery mentality.

One does not have to stir around the American Negro problem for very long before sex rears its ugly head: as potent a psychological force as in the New Left movement already discussed.*   This issue is an incredible psychic tangle with threads of white-man jealousy of alleged Negro virility, puritanical horror and guilt at cross-racial illicit relationships and belief that the "white race" should be kept pure, unadulterated by miscegenation. In the American South, lynchings were frequently the "punishment" for a Negro having or being alleged to have had sexual relations with a white woman; marriage between the races is forbidden by law in South Africa; while the Nazis tried to establish a eugenic policy of procreating a pure race by encouraging breeding between people of "good Aryan stock". The belief that all Negroes have a voracious sexual appetite is an example of the psychological process known as stereotyping. This is the technique of asserting that all people of a particular group, racial or other, are possessed of a particular quality: Jews are miserly, Chinese are inscrutable, English are cold and reserved. These supposed characteristics have even slipped into phrases of everyday usage so that one is said

* See above pp. 42-43.

to take Dutch courage or to identify the nigger in the woodpile. Individual personality is smothered by such blanket descriptions.

During the above discussion of three major bases of racialism, it has rather been assumed that the "race problem" is synonymous with the "colour problem". Prejudice against the negroid people is, in fact, far more deeply rooted than against other racial groups. A number of possible explanations have been canvassed for this: the eighteenth-century biologists' assertion that the black man occupied the lowest place on the evolutionary tree; the slavery background of the American and Caribbean Negroes; the stereotyping process; the obvious ease with which white and black can be distinguished. Some commentators have, however, felt these explanations to be rather fragile and have sought deeper psychological explanations in the symbolic equation of black with evil.

Having identified the components of racialism, one may pose the specific question, "How racialist is Britain?" This is a question which is of more than insular interest, for Britain has been noted in the past for its toleration of minority groups, whether they be racial, national or religious, and occupies a special position as the mother of the multiracial Commonwealth. The incidence of racially-induced violence has happily been very limited, the riots in Notting Hill and Nottingham in 1958 being the only serious outbursts. Moreover, the legislation of the 1960s to limit immigration can hardly be rated as ideologically racial, rather as a pragmatic response in order to damp down communal tension. The most passionate reaction to the race problem that has gained widespread publicity has emanated from Enoch Powell. In a mounting campaign of articles and speeches, he has foretold disaster for the country if the number of coloured inhabitants is not cut back, eventually, indeed, reaching the point where he advocated repatriation. "We must be mad," he declared in a speech in Birmingham in 1968, "literally mad as a nation to be permitting the annual inflow of 50,000 dependants . . . it is like watching a nation busily engaged in heaping up its own funeral pyre."[31] The National Front took up the theme.

Mr. Powell, however, vehemently denies that he is a racialist. His argument is a very simple one: racial groups, like oil and water, just do not mix; everyone will therefore be happier if they are kept apart — precisely the same argument as that produced by the exponents of Black Nationalism in the USA and of apartheid in South Africa. Logically this is a proposition distinct from the strictly racialist idea that certain races are inferior or should be treated as such. But, in politics logic does not always prevail, and pragmatic arguments just for segregation can lead on in practice to the racialist denial of human rights.

Few people would wish all racial differences to be levelled out: a world of khaki cosmopolitans would in all probability be a culturally poorer planet than the piebald one we inhabit today. Nevertheless, toleration and justice must prevail if human misery is not to be magnified by racialist ideology. For once racialism gets a grip there is no escaping. An individual may avoid nationalist persecution by adopting the language and customs of the aggressive group. But no one can change his race. However lily-white the skin of a South African, if it is discovered that a grandparent was Bantu, he is labelled — and condemned — as a Coloured. It is the inexorability of racialism that makes it a frightening creed.

Technocracy
All the vast social changes promised by the class revolution and by racial domination shrink before the incredible potential of science, especially in its applied form of technology. But whether this is a potential for good or for evil is a matter open to considerable debate. There is an air of doom about much of the discussion surrounding the impact of science on contemporary society, a feeling that in the technological revolution mankind represents the crushed forces of the *ancien regime.* And the problem becomes a political one because the issues facing us concern the control of science and technology by the politicians, administrators and the ordinary citizens, and, in turn, the control of these people by science and technology. In the words of *The Times*:

Many advanced states are experiencing, within themselves, the same kind of gap between public opinion and the machinery of government. A paradox of the modern technological society is revealed: the society creates problems so complex that they can be handled only by those with specialist skill and intricate knowledge, and at the same time it produces people who are in general more highly educated and inquiring than previous generations. It centralises decision-making but spreads the desire to make decisions. How can democracy, in this predicament, satisfy both the need for greater efficiency and the need for wider participation? [32]

This is just one hint of the ambivalent confusion with which we view science: as a source of both enlightenment and evil. In political terms, science both generates progress and freedom and strengthens authority and arcane bureaucratic mystiques. The basic political danger is the technical ease with which governments can now control and manipulate a population and the unavoidable surrender of decision-making to the scientifically proficient "expert". The communications and cybernetics revolutions have placed immense potential power into the hands of the government. Even the electorate in an outwardly democratic country like the USA, as Eugene Burdick showed in his novel *The 480*, can be manipulated by skilful use of computer and television. In the opinion of Charles Reich, indeed, the technologically mature United States is already "a mindless juggernaut, destroying the environment, obliterating human values, and assuming domination over the lives and minds of its subjects." [33] Democracy and technology, in this view, are incompatible: democracy is government by the good sense of the common man; technocracy is government by the dictates of scientific knowledge. The common man is ignorant in an age in which knowledge is power. However, the situation is complex. Who wields this scientifically based power? Perhaps the politicians, as has been assumed so far; perhaps the bureaucrats as will be discussed in a little while; but perhaps not the government at all. The growth of massive, supranational industrial businesses with personnel and wealth in excess of some nation-states, raises the spectre of considerable political power being exercised by people outside the whole government apparatus altogether.

And yet, for all the difficulties raised by these matters, the root political issue with which the development of science and technology has faced us is the role of the expert. Traditionally, politicians have possessed only the general skills of their trade, like speech-making, and bureaucrats, the general capacity to administer. These men now have to make decisions which can only be responsibly made if founded on scientific understanding. The Fulton Committee condemned the amateurism of the British civil service on grounds of inefficiency; earlier, in his Godkin Lectures, C.P. Snow had deplored the lack of scientific education among men who literally hold the lives of millions of people in their hands. "One of the bizarre features of any advanced industrial society in our times," he declared, " is that the cardinal choices have to be made by a handful of men: in secret: and, at least in legal form, by men who cannot have a first-hand knowledge of what those choices depend upon or what their results may be." [34]

Both Lords Snow and Fulton argued for a more appropriate education for our masters. However, scientific knowledge is expanding at such a rate that it is impracticable to think in terms of any individual combining both political and scientific expertise, rather like Plato's ruling Guardians. The technical expert will always be needed. The danger is that men in positions of authority will live in awe of this "new priesthood" (the phrase is Ralph Lapp's) as Churchill was in awe of Cherwell and Stalin perhaps of Lysenko. In such conditions the scientist has power, immense political power, without responsibility – an abuse of prerogative far more sinister than that enjoyed by any harlot or Press baron who might have been in Mr Baldwin's mind when he coined the phrase. Interestingly, it was left to that most amateur of modern politicians, President Eisenhower, to raise the alarm against the "unwarranted influence" of the "military-industrial complex" and the "scientific-technological élite" in his farewell address in 1961.

There are some who view the emergence of the expert with a cooler detachment. The emergence to effective political power of the expert, whether he be bureaucrat, technocrat or business executive, has been identified by some social scientists as both a fact of life and a development to be favoured. This is the ideology of technocracy. The supposed benefits are twofold. First, there is efficiency. If politics is a science and if government should be conducted rationally, decisions should be placed in the hands of those with the technical expertise. By this argument politics is equated with administration, administration with efficiency, and efficiency with technical knowledge. What is more, and this is the second argument, if we leave matters in the capable hands of the expert, we shall avoid the wasteful bitterness of ideological conflict. It is not a new argument in essence. Two and a half centuries ago Alexander Pope expressed the thought in his *Essay on Man*:

> For forms of government let fools contest;
> Whate'er is best administered is best.

Today we have social scientists rather than poets to bring us the message; and it has been given a much sharper edge by recent technological developments. One of the most celebrated works in this field is James Burnham's *The Managerial Revolution* (1943). He has argued that both capitalist and Communist societies are being replaced by a new, managerial society. The "managers" are coming to form a new class in the modern, industrial state, are acquiring such influence that they are taking over effective control. Thus, instead of becoming increasingly different and hostile, capitalist and Communist states are, in fact, converging as the managers – technocrats and top executives – render the established ideologies obsolete.

There is a real danger of assuming that problems can be solved by more scientific "know how", just as there is a danger of slipping into thinking that science and technology are by themselves good or bad. The truth is, of course, that it is the *use* of technology that is good or evil and that problems have to be met by establishing priorities. And in these processes scientific knowledge itself can be of little assistance. Decisions about *how* the results of technology are to be used are political questions because they are questions about ends; science is about means. There is still therefore the residual question of how we need to adjust our political processes to make science our servant and not our master. Science is not a panacea, and the modern Prometheus will be chastised if he acts as if it were. Under appropriate political control science can yet improve the quality of life for many. Political man, be he politician, civil servant or citizen, must adapt to the new scientific age, learn to exploit the values of the new knowledge and techniques and guard against the dangers. In what circumstances should a thermonuclear weapon be used? What action should the government take to curb the rising population? How much countryside should be transformed into the concrete jungle of town and motorway? These are political questions which modern technology is posing with ever-pressing insistence. It is likely that judicious answers will be forthcoming only if the traditional relationship between the voter, the bureaucrat and the politician are revised: they cannot be left to the technocrat alone.

Note on the New Left
When this book was written it was customary to label the extreme left-wing movements described on pages 39–43 as the New Left. This term no longer has currency and should be used only in an historical sense about the situation in the late 1960s. The term Far Left is now sometimes used for the groups holding these beliefs.

4 Organisation Within the Political Unit

The distribution of power

Politics is about power. On individuals, as Acton believed, it may indeed have a malign influence; but for society at large, whether it is benign or malignant depends on the amount that is wielded. Like radiation, large doses can be deadly while properly administered small doses can be indispensable in curing the cancer of social disintegration. One has only to read *1984* and *Lord of the Flies* to recognise the two extreme conditions. In a famous survey, [1] Aristotle analysed political systems on the bases of the numbers exercising power and the quality of the resultant government. The pattern is a sixfold classification into good monarchy, bad tyranny; good aristocracy, bad oligarchy; good polity (mixed government), bad ochlocracy (mob rule) or democracy. The frame of reference used in this chapter is not so much numbers of politicians as the intensity of concentration of power.

Concentration of power is a particularly urgent issue in contemporary society. Especially in highly industrialised states, social and political efficiency render wide exercise of power by a central bureaucratised government necessary, while bureaucratic, police and communications systems render the massive concentration of power possible. At the same time, more widespread education makes an increasing proportion of the population resentful at the crushing of individual personality and initiative. Exponents of the minimisation of power arm themselves with the ideology of anarchism; totalitarianism is the ideology of the power worshipper; in between these extremes the democrat advocates the exercise of power, but diffused and controlled.

Anarchism

Clad in broad-brimmed hat and concealing cloak, armed with a dagger and fused bomb, the traditional anarchist stalks our imaginations in caricatured form. The image was created by the activities of certain anarchists in the nineteenth century, but it is kept alive by sabotage incidents undertaken from time to time by groups like the Angry Brigade in Britain, who succeeded in 1971 in gaining publicity for their hostility to contemporary society by planting a bomb at the house of Mr. Robert Carr, then Secretary of State for Employment. The use of violence is just a publicity stunt (or symbolic act, if you wish); it is not central to the anarchist doctrine, indeed many anarchists whole-heartedly reject violence.

Any attempt to provide a simple analysis of anarchism is rather like viewing a pointilliste painting: the closer you look, the more the picture breaks up into its component dots. After all, the development and acceptance of a coherent doctrine requires a discipline that is the very negation of anarchist individualism. A succinct definition has, however, been provided by one of the leading contemporary exponents of the idea, Paul Goodman. Referring to the student demonstrators of 1968 (the black flag of anarchism flew side-by-side over the Sorbonne with the red Marxist flag), he has written:

> They believe in local power, community development, rural reconstruction, decentralist organisation .... They prefer a simpler standard of living ... they do not trust the due process of administrators and are quick to resort to direct action and civil disobedience. All this adds up to the community Anarchism of Kropotkin, the resistance Anarchism of Malatesta, the agitational Anarchism of Bakunin. [2]

The last sentence reminds us that anarchism has nineteenth-century intellectual origins of considerable distinction, and much of modern thinking is rooted in this tradition. In order to examine the theory of anarchism it is convenient to pose four questions: What does anarchism reject? What does it positively propose? Who are the contemporary exponents of anarchism? How should one assess the doctrine?

Although we are starting this analysis with a statement of what anarchism rejects, it is worth emphasising that the doctrine does not dismiss all forms of social organisation: anarchism does not advocate anarchy in the popular sense of the word. What anarchism does reject primarily is the power apparatus of the modern state. He who wields political power abuses it; he who is controlled by political power has his individuality stifled. The major aim of the anarchist is, therefore, to weaken and diffuse institutionalised power. For the ordinary citizen this power takes the visible form of the unholy trinity of the bureaucracy, the police and the law. Bureaucracy means the exercise of power by remote control, it means priority for the "expert" over the individual — all this is anathema to the anarchist. Bureaucracy, moreover, makes the anarchist feel particularly frustrated since it is difficult to personalise his resentment (unless the administrative rub is at the essentially local level, as has occurred, for example, with student rage at the impersonality of many large universities). Personal confrontation is easiest with the police, of course. Furthermore, clashes between demonstrators and "pigs" are always good for headlines. The function of the police, as the anarchist sees it, is not so much the maintenance of law and order as the preservation of state power. That the police in some countries are all too ready to use brutal methods to sustain the status quo seemed to be demonstrated in the boisterous events of 1968 attending the Democratic Party Convention in Chicago and the student-inspired revolt in Paris. If, moreover, the anarchists believe that the police are to be personally abused and their authority denied because they are no more than the instruments of state power, the legal code which they are employed to uphold is no more sacrosanct. For the anarchist the law is only a complex attempt to justify the very system they reject. It might be thought that some political systems are less obnoxious to the anarchists than others, but this is not really so. A democratic constitution is just as repugnant, just as tyrannical in essence as a dictatorship. Kropotkin was quite blunt about this: "The theory of the 'balancing of powers' and 'control of authorities' is a hypocritical formula, invented by those who have seized power, to make the 'sovereign people', whom they despise, believe that the people themselves are governing." [3]

Once one has thrown overboard the modern state system, a whole string of connected institutions inevitably tumbles out with it. For example, just as law is perceived as an instrument of the repressive state, so the moral code of society is similarly interpreted and rejected. Private property is considered a form of theft, a proposition formulated by Proudhon in the nineteenth century and reiterated most recently by Abbie Hoffman, the Yippie leader. War is objectionable, not because of any fundamental belief in the sanctity of human life but because organisation for hostilities results in the further concentration of state power. Similarly, urbanisation and the effects of technology are disliked because these trends reinforce the anonymity of life and the power of impersonal forces. The list is pretty formidable, but an appendix must yet be added. Marxism rejects the state system and interprets the law, morality and so forth as mere reflections of the dominant social forces. Nevertheless, Marxism and anarchism must not be confused: indeed, since the very earliest exposition of his ideas by Marx, the two movements have been at loggerheads. Marxism stands for a class and a party solidarity and thus a concentration of power quite as hostile to the anarchist ideal as the capitalist state. There have been alliances, it is true, but they have been pragmatic, temporary and sometimes painful. The experience of the Spanish Civil War, as Orwell showed in his *Homage to Catalonia,* was justification enough for the anarchist's distrust of the Communists.

Anarchism would tear down the edifice of the modern state and, indeed, uproot some of its very foundations. What would the anarchist architects build in its place? Inevitably, the basic premise is that power should be exercised in the most attenuated form possible. Some form of social organisation is recognised as being inevitable; but whatever associations are thrown up to meet this need should be voluntary, functional, temporary and small. Voluntary, to prevent the imposition of power; functional, to prevent the spread of power; temporary and small, to prevent the consolidation of power. Since the complete destruction of the present state system would lead to utter chaos, anarchists propose the devolution of authority within any given state to a federation of virtually autonomous local communities. Each commune would be self-regulating and property would be shared in common. In the words of Jerry Rubin, an American Yippie:

> We have to create our own communist islands within a capitalist sea, controlling our own art, setting up free stores, free food centers, free medical and mental clinics, free legal services, bail funds, crash pads, music co-ops, free garages, switchboards, housing collectives. [4]

The idea of local communes is a strong theme in left-wing thought, pre-dating Marx's socialism in the works of the British Robert Owen and the Frenchman Proudhon, for example, in the early nineteenth century. Just as the drab inhumanity of the Industrial Revolution generated these ideas, so there has been a widespread reaction against the regimentation of contemporary technological society, so that even the Young Liberals expound the communitarian ideas of anarchism. The idea of communalism raises, indeed, fundamental questions about the efficacy of our present democratic system[5]. Anarchism appeals currently to two distinct groups — students and workers. The youthful generation of students tend to be more utopian in their programmes. Among industrial workers, syndicalism has been a popular and reasonably practical form of community organisation. This is the doctrine that proposes the seizure of the control of industry by the trade unions and the development of the unions as the community units favoured by anarchist theory. Anarcho-syndicalist ideas enjoyed considerable favour in Europe in this century up to the time of the Spanish Civil War and experienced a brief recrudescence in France in 1968.

Implicit in all that has been said is, of course, a simpler, more natural life-style than is common in industrial societies. There is more than a touch of William Morris about anarchism. Craftsmanship, indeed artistic and scientific creativity generally, absorb human energies in the anarchist society, rather than the destructive pursuit and exercise of political power. It is no accident that the artist Herbert Read and the biologist Alex Comfort have been leading exponents of anarchism in England in recent years. Non-political are more significant than political values.

But although one must turn to writers like Read and Comfort for modern contributions to anarchist thought of any quality, the most vigorous anarchist activity has occurred in the USA — perhaps not surprisingly since it combines the maximum of industrialised conformity with the maximum opportunity to express nonconformist views. Exponents of the Alternative Society have come in three waves. The first to arrive on the American scene were the Beatniks in the 1950s, their philosophy of alienation expounded by the poet Allen Ginsberg. However, their drab withdrawal from society was not to be a permanent characteristic of the protest scene. Colour and public-eye-catching antics were injected by the Hippies — the loud and flashy flower-people. But Hippies were psychedelic rather than political. Positive political campaigning was combined with the vivid life-style by a new movement that had emerged by 1967 called the "Yippies" (Youth International Party). As their magazine, *Ramparts*, declared, "Our life style — acid, long hair, freaky clothes, pot, rock music, sex — is the Revolution." [6]   Like the Pixies — a similar movement that has created some sensation in Amsterdam — the Yippies used public demonstration hoaxes to effect disruption of social services and to satirise the established system. Tactics of shock and mockery replace violence. The most famous were the antics of the Yippies in Chicago in the summer of 1968 during the Democratic Party convention. They held their own convention and solemnly nominated a pig as presidential candidate. At the same time they forced the authorities to mount guard over the reservoirs by threatening to "turn on" the whole population of the city by adding LSD to the water supply!

How is one to assess anarchism? A massive childish hoax; a sinister threat to the foundations of civil society; or a genuine search for a less hypocritical form of society? Clearly one must distinguish between the anarchism of the drop-out and the anarchism of the revolutionary; between anarchism as an alternative way of life within an unreformed society and anarchism as a revolutionary transformation of the whole of society. Judgment must be personal, but three important factors may be borne in mind while making the judgment. Anarchism should not be assessed by dramatic displays; the heart of the doctrine does not lie there. Secondly, a major restructuring of society into a network of primitive communes is sheer utopianism — neither practicable nor, probably for most people, very congenial. But finally, it must not be forgotten that the individualist tone of anarchist thinking can act as an important regulator on more realistic social thought. If the essence of beneficent political thinking is a cool appraisal of all contributions rather than the fervent acceptance of a single, all-embracing ideology, then perhaps even anarchism has something positive to contribute; after all, there is something of the anarchist in all of us who shrink from the competitive rat-race and the tyranny of the telephone, typewriter and train time-table.

Totalitarianism

The anarchist sees the options starkly as man or leviathan and firmly chooses man. The totalitarian, wielding the massive power that the anarchist abhors, legitimises that power by appeal to class or racial ideology and creates a monstrous state against which the individual shrivels to insignificance. The Europe of the 1930s and '40s recorded its horror in the literature of Orwell, Huxley and Koestler as it witnessed the shrinking of the German nation to a vast army of gesticulating puppets and the freezing of the Russian people into paralysed terror.

The realisation of the absolute nature of totalitarian control has faded somewhat from our thoughts. Not least of the qualities of Solzhenitsyn is that he continues to irritate that part of the mind that harbours the fear and thus sustains our consciousness of the danger.

For totalitarianism is not just a longer word for dictatorship, autocracy or tyranny. Many forms of authoritarian control have been exercised in mankind's history; totalitarianism is unique in the very completeness of its power and its fanatical obsession with an ideal. Totalitarianism is no mere repression of opposition in a purely negative way, it is a positive urge to create a utopia. Totalitarianism is ideology *par excellence*: the individual must be totally committed to the regime, no particle of his life or thought can be allowed to be discordant with the ideology. The whole of life is woven into the political pattern:

> The whole framework of our social life [wrote the Soviet music critic, Olesha] is very closely knit together, comrades. In the life and activity of our State nothing moves or develops independently. . . . If I do not agree with the Party in a single point, the whole picture of life must be dimmed for me, because all parts, all details of the picture are bound together and arise out of each other, therefore there can be no single false line anywhere. [7]

Thus it has come about in pursuit of racial purity in Nazi Germany and of the domination of the proletariat in Stalinist Russia that a complete totalitarian structure was raised; and in the name of the same principle Afrikaner South Africa and Maoist China have displayed similar tendencies. The starting points are quite different, as are the intentions, and some would therefore not wish to bracket them together; but the end-products are remarkably alike. To the totalitarian no art is valid unless it is a mirror to the ideology. "There is, in fact," declared Mao, "no such thing as art for art's sake, art that stands above classes, art that is detached from or independent of politics." [8] In the Soviet Union a considerable campaign was mounted by Zhdanov in the immediate postwar period to persecute writers, artists and musicians who did not conform to the canons of "socialist realism". And whatever one might think about the provocations of modern art forms in the "decadent west" there really is a limit to the artistic potential that can be extorted from a cheery-faced miner who has exceeded his production norm. Nor is sport, that most fraternal of all human activities, immune from totalitarian control. In South Africa players of different colours are not allowed to participate in the same teams; while not so many years ago the success of a Chinese table-tennis team was seriously attributed to the aggressive tactics they had absorbed through reading the *Thoughts* of Chairman Mao. Science — the pursuit of absolute truth and understanding — it might be argued, must surely escape the totalitarian tentacles. But no. Stalin felt quite competent to use Marxist principles to judge the hypotheses of the Soviet biologist Lysenko. Thus present activity is controlled in order to shape future society. But time is a continuum and the past is not allowed to sleep or be forgotten: history is rewritten in order to provide the regime with an impeccable ancestry. The totalitarian clothes himself in the armour of relentless logic and scrupulously avoids baring any chink before opponent or sceptic.

Total control cannot be said to exist unless the whole population unquestioningly accepts the regime. The totalitarian sets about this with incredible thoroughness by deploying all the sophisticated techniques of indoctrination that the twentieth century has so ingeniously devised. The amazing success with which totalitarian leaders have mobilised popular opinion can be explained in two ways: the passive receptiveness of the mass of the people to the ideology and the active propaganda policy of the regime. Totalitarian systems are marked by a surprising lack of resistance. The bulk of the people are willing to accept the regime, perhaps even welcome it, because they are in psychological need of firm leadership: the Germans accepted Hitler after utter economic collapse; the Russians, Stalin, after revolution and civil war; the Chinese, Mao, after an intolerably long period of chaos marked by revolution, civil war, foreign invasion and warlordism. The relative stability of the British economy and political system may explain the complete failure of authoritarian movements like the British Union of Fascists to secure any real grip on the country.

It needs only the propagandist with his wide range of dramatic wizardry to transform willing supporters into eager fanatics. Mass enthusiasm is whipped up by organising youth movements, staging mass rallies and manipulating the mass media. Youth is important for its enthusiasm, pliability and investment for the future; mass rallies are important as visible demonstrations of the size and enthusiasm of the support; control of the media is important for the art of gentle brainwashing. By these means massive support is drummed up for the leader and the cause which he symbolises, while solidarity is further hardened by the identification of a common enemy. This whole process may be conveniently illustrated by reference to the recent situation in China. The totalitarian bent of Maoist Communism became particularly evident during the Cultural Revolution of the mid-1960s. Schools and institutions of higher education were shut down in June 1966 and many of their students recruited into the militant adolescent Red Guard movement; in August an incredible meeting of an estimated one million people was held in Peking; while the doctrine of the Cultural Revolution was propagated by posters pasted on to almost every available wall-space. The result of all these activities? A popular support that is more widespread and more committed than that enjoyed by so-called democratic governments. It is a myth that totalitarian regimes sit on vast populations who would rise up if only they could; rather are the regimes buoyed up by an effervescent populace.

As in all authoritarian governments, leadership is a key factor in totalitarianism: both in providing a symbolic hero-figure and an organisational framework for the ideology to work through it goes far to explain the successes of these regimes. The exaltation of the leader is an important device: he provides a focus of loyalty and the source of doctrinal wisdom. The process reached its most perfect form in the personality cult of Stalin, lampooned by Orwell and denounced by Khrushchev. The omniscience and omnipotence of Stalin was satirised in *Animal Farm:*

> In his speeches, Squealer would talk with the tears rolling down his cheeks of Napoleon's wisdom, the goodness of his heart, and the deep love he bore to all animals everywhere. . . . It had become usual to give Napoleon the credit for every successful achievement and every stroke of good fortune. You would often hear one hen remark to another, "Under the guidance of our Leader, Comrade Napoleon, I have laid five eggs in six days." [9]

The nauseating obsequiousness demanded by Stalin, the brutal tyrant, was dramatically denounced by Khrushchev three years after the dictator's death.

In fact, of course, no leader is omnipotent; the efficiency of his government and the very primacy of his position depend on the ability and loyalty of a select cadre of followers. The function of this élite is to be a model of excellence for the whole people to copy; "whips" to ensure, by education or force, that the mass of the people are obedient to the regime; spurs to dedicated work; and loyal defenders of the indisputable genius of the leader. It is through the recognised vital importance of such a select band that totalitarian systems elevate the party to a position of supreme influence. The party machine is the means by which the cadres are selected, recruited and set to work. This élite must, of course, be doctrinally pure and dedicated to the cause and to the leader. Preliminary selection must sift out as far as possible applicants with blemishes of intellect or character. Nevertheless, difficulties do arise within the party: personal ambition, doctrinal heresy, questioning of the leader can all lead to fractures in the monolithic structure. It is scarcely surprising, therefore, that one of the features common to totalitarian regimes is the purge — the Night of the Long Knives, the Moscow Show Trials, the Cultural Revolution: a purification of the party apparatus or, if you will, the annihilation of the opponents of the dictator.

Purging of party members is but one facet of the general policy of Terror — the cold-blooded and bloody manipulation of the fear of the whole population in order to destroy individuality and achieve their abject submission to the government and its ideology by fostering the belief in the omnipotence of the system. Terror is institutionalised fear. Opposition becomes unthinkable: life becomes an eager struggle to gain acceptance as devotees of the ideology; for those whose class or race renders this impossible, their lot is a resigned despair.

Terror has two main weapons, both of which were honed to perfection in Stalinist Russia: the political and concentration or labour camps. And it must be emphasised that their functions were general as well as specific — not merely to track down and punish opponents of the regime, but to sustain a constant atmosphere of fear; to "encourage" those who are not taken in by the propaganda machine. Propaganda and terror are the two complementary sides of the totalitarian coin. The political police organisation under Stalin (variously named OGPU, NKVD, MVD) developed immense power with its administrative, economic and military machinery. Virtually no one was safe. At the whim of Stalin or the police chief (Beria in the postwar period) even the most senior party men could be whisked from their homes, accused of quite fantastic trumped-up charges and forced into public confessions of guilt. The arbitrariness and secretiveness of the arrest procedure was a vital psychological technique to promote the edginess of uncertainty throughout the country; the public announcement of confession was important as publicity for the omnipotence of the police system. For maximum effect, confessions of the guilty had to be publicised; their fate kept mysteriously secret. The labour camp system achieved the second of these desired results. It was a most efficient instrument for ensuring the suppression of the most stubborn opponents of the regime. Ignorance as to their fate prevented an aura of martyrdom from developing; being herded together in subhuman conditions destroyed the individual's desire for anything but sheer survival. The intense concentration of effort and ingenuity to acquire an extra morsel of food or an added degree of warmth is vividly portrayed, for example, in Solzhenitsyn's little cameo, *One Day in the Life of Ivan Denisovitch*. The individual is crushed beneath the overwhelming weight of the leviathan. Control is total. In the words of the French commentator, David Rousset:

> Nothing is more terrible than these processions of human beings going like dummies to their death. The man who sees this says to himself: "For them to be thus reduced, what power must be concealed in the hands of the masters," and he turns away, full of bitterness but defeated. [10]

In practical terms, totalitarianism concerns itself most obviously with the domination of the individual within any given society. However, the emphasis on totality extends in theory to a domination that is unbounded by time or space. The historical process is conceived as inevitable; the ideologically favoured race, class or revolutionary society will come to enjoy a globally dominant role, however long it might take for it to reach the pinnacle. The prospect that the process could stretch for some distance into the future diminishes the importance of the present: even human suffering on a gigantic scale is rendered insignificant in comparison with the aeons of utopia for which this misery is conceived as being but a necessary preparation. Indeed, one of the most terrifying features of totalitarianism is the grim, utter conviction of the exponents of the doctrine that they are right, that ultimately their ideology must vanquish all opponents and reign as the supreme interpretation and organiser of the human social condition. As Khrushchev confidently said to President Eisenhower, "We will bury you."

Totalitarianism clearly reached its apogee in the 1930s and '40s in Hitlerite Germany and Stalinist Russia. How far does totalitarianism

exist today? Nazism was, of course, killed in 1945, but Stalinism lived on and indeed spawned parasites in eastern Europe. Life was kept as taut as a fiddle-string. Then, in 1953, Stalin died and the tension was relaxed. And yet, even if the full panoply of totalitarianism no longer exists, sufficient of its atmosphere remains for one to hesitate before discarding the term. The retention of a powerful repressive police system has been advertised since the early 1960s by the censored literature that has been smuggled out of the country and the known practice of incarcerating opponents of the regime in lunatic asylums as well as labour camps. Valeriy Tarsis has denounced "the hypocrisy of the device which enabled the authorities to claim that there were no political prisoners but only 'lunatics' receiving 'treatment' ".[11]
The relaxation of the tension has been termed the thaw, and a similar warmth has been enjoyed in the states of eastern Europe; yet again, as in the Soviet Union, jagged remnants of icy totalitarianism are still in evidence. But perhaps of greatest importance is to question how far China is a totalitarian regime. As far as evidence allows one to judge, the imposition and confirming of Communist ideology of the Maoist brand have been achieved without bloodshed and violence on anything like the scale experienced under Nazism and Stalinism. Nevertheless, the other criteria of totalitarianism are well satisfied: it has a utopian ideology, by propaganda and brainwashing techniques it has secured considerable popular support – indeed considerable dedication by many, and the whole movement was topped by a messianic leader. If totalitarianism consists of the regimentation of a whole people in support of a creed by a dedicated group on behalf of an inspiring leader, then the Chinese People's Republic warrants the label.

This is not to make the judgment that people in China are more wretched now than under the Nationalist or Imperial regimes. Indeed the reverse is in all probability true. Should one conclude, then, that there is nothing particularly objectionable about totalitarianism as an ideology and style of government? The answer must be an unequivocal "no". Totalitarianism may provide a sense of purpose and economic advancement at an actual human price that is not excessive (however that can be calculated). But the potential price, actually realised in Nazi Germany and Stalinist Russia, is exorbitant. Totalitarianism must be rejected as an aberrant doctrine of the twentieth century. It politicises the whole of life and degrades the human being to an expendable unit. Human dignity, human life itself, is devoured by the great totalitarian maw to feed its insatiable appetite for power.

The nature of democracy

Democracy, on the other hand, is restrained power. A snappy definition such as this, however, does not get us very far. Is it, for example, really no more than mere political technique? This is the view of Professor Schumpeter, who defined democracy as "that institutional arrangement for arriving at political decisions in which individuals acquire the power to decide by means of a competitive struggle for the people's vote." [12] And it is a view certainly not confined to the academic political scientist. Harold Macmillan, an old parliamentary trouper, has been reported declaring that, "if people want a sense of purpose they should get it from their archbishops. They should not hope to receive it from their politicians." [13] But is democracy just a matter of ballot-boxes? Is there not something deeper to the preservation of the inalienable rights of life, liberty and the pursuit of happiness, or whatever formulation you choose to epitomise democracy? Democracy is indeed a series of political techniques to balance state power and individual licence; but the urge to achieve this balance presupposes certain qualities and conditions of life to be desirable, namely the fullest opportunity for human development consonant with stable, orderly social organisation. Neither the automaton of totalitarianism nor the free-wheeling spirit of anarchism fit the democratic mood. Political process and life-style are mutually necessary features of democracy.

How are we to recognise what is democratic? It is a style of government frequently considered to have originated (in modern times) in the Atlantic area and still to be fundamentally restricted to that geographical portion of the globe. Britain, the USA and France, so the argument runs, provide the archetypal patterns which are being nobly followed by a few wise heirs to the tradition like India.[14] This view is considered too blinkered by C.B. Macpherson, who, in a series of well-known lectures, [15] has argued that the Communist and the Third World single-party systems of government have as much right to the title of democratic, indeed are potentially closer to "the original notion of democracy as rule by and for the poor and oppressed". [16] (A notion, which, we may note, was tarred with the terrorist Jacobin brush from the 1790s, and therefore feared rather than lauded by many nineteenth-century politicians.) We shall need to test this thesis. For this purpose we need a yardstick. It is proposed to adopt a fairly simple one here: that the essentials of democracy are freedom, equality and participation: that the full development of the human personality requires freedom and equality and that participation is a necessary method of ensuring that the government does not deny them.

Freedom

Defining the relationship between freedom and democracy is rather like drawing mathematical sets. One may describe two circles to represent the two concepts but neither is the one synonymous with the other nor does the one totally contain the other. For freedom, while being an absolutely essential constituent of democracy, is not the whole of democracy; moreover, freedom may be enjoyed in non-democratic regimes. For example, a regime that constrained personal liberty by engaging in arbitrary arrests could scarcely be called democratic; while considerable liberty did exist in eighteenth- and early nineteenth-century England before the achievement of a democratic political system. Liberty has been a rallying cry for revolutionaries for centuries, whether they be struggling for political, social or national freedom. The great Statue of Liberty was erected in New York to remind immigrants of the fundamental principle on which American society was founded; more recently *uhuru* (freedom) has become the best known Swahili word outside Africa. And the whole tone of post-war thinking about the desirable society that should replace fascism was shaped by Roosevelt's definition of the Four Freedoms:

> In the future days which we seek to make secure [he declared in January 1941], we look forward to a world founded upon four essential human freedoms.
> The first is freedom of speech and expression. . . .
> The second is freedom of every person to worship God in his own way. . . .
> The third is freedom from want. . . .
> The fourth is freedom from fear. . . .[17]

It will be clear from a cursory reading of this declaration that the American President was using the term "freedom" in two different ways − both freedom *from* undesirable constraints and freedom *to* pursue desired ends. A parallel distinction, between "negative" and "positive" liberty, was the subject of Sir Isaiah Berlin's controversial inaugural lecture, in which he concluded that

> Pluralism, with the measure of "negative" liberty that it entails, seems to me a truer and more humane ideal than the goals of those who seek in the great, disciplined, authoritarian structures the ideal of "positive" self-mastery by classes, or peoples, or the whole of mankind. It is truer, because it does at least recognize the fact that human goals are many, not all of them commensurable, and in perpetual rivalry with one another. [18]

Democratic societies are clearly characterised by a whole range of negative freedoms: freedom from discrimination, persecution and arrest for holding or propagating certain beliefs and opinions. But "positive" freedom — freedom to pursue a life-style by not only adopting it but imposing it upon others — is, as Berlin argues, a positive danger. Freedom must be tempered with toleration if it is to be worthy of the name and to contribute to the construction of democracy. Liberty without tolerance is nigh to tyranny; tolerance without liberty is vacuous. Tolerance — "the degree to which we accept things of which we disapprove" [19] — is vital to democracy for two reasons: to prevent the domination of the minority by the majority and to encourage that diversity of beliefs and behaviours without which man cannot fulfil his human potential, for we have come rightly to expect our democratic political institutions to provide the context in which individualism may flower.

Diversity and freedom to give it full rein must in practice allow for a range of choice of rulers. One can hardly be said to be politically free if one is stuck with a single set of politicians: this leads to security of power and hence irresponsibility and a lack of alternative policies. In consequence many writers have emphasised the vital importance for democracy of the existence of an alternative government — an opposition (described by Henry Mayo as "the litmus-paper test of democracy." [20]) And yet there are forceful arguments for considering *single*-party systems as democracies, provided, as in some African states, there is genuine debate and contest within the party. [21]

Ensuring that the citizen has a choice of rulers is one way of securing freedom. There are two other well-established principles directed to the same end that need to be mentioned: these are the rule of law and the separation of powers. The essence of the rule of law is that citizens should be treated equally without favour or discrimination and that the law should not be operated arbitrarily: laws should not be put into effect with uneven severity or retrospectively. The main threat of arbitrary action has seemed to come in Britain in recent years largely from the maladministration of government departments against whom the ordinary mills of the law grind slowly or not at all. As a result a Parliamentary Commissioner for Administration (or Ombudsman) was appointed in 1967 to investigate complaints deriving from this quarter.

The classic constitutional guarantee of freedom, since the time of Locke certainly, has been the so-called separation of powers. Government is conceived as consisting of the Executive, the Legislature and Judiciary. Freedom might be endangered if any of them, and especially the Executive, acquired a dominating position over the rest. In drawing up their constitution, the American revolutionaries opted for a fully-fledged system of separation — hence the inability, for example, of members of the US cabinet to be members of Congress. This regulation is quite contrary to the British practice. The American system derives from a misreading of British eighteenth-century practice and Montesquieu's comment upon it. "In order that power shall not be abused," he wrote in *L'Esprit des lois*, "it is necessary that, by the arrangement of things, power shall check power." "They overlap and limit one another," explained Alfred Cobban. "The system he is describing is one of checks and balances, not of rigid separation." [22] The American and British systems of government will repay further comparison. The American constitution has gone the farthest to provide machinery for the diffusion and separation of power — by the federal arrangement of devolution of power from the centre as well as the separation of powers at the centre. In contrast, the British cabinet system achieves, in Bagehot's words, "the close union, the nearly complete fusion of the executive and the legislative powers" [23] — that is a *concentration* of power. Yet, paradoxically, in so far as there are fears about an over-concentration of power in Britain, it is because of the putative development of an American presidential style of government by recent prime ministers, especially seen in the development of the Wilson cult of personality from 1964 to 1970.

Equality

"Men are born and remain free and equal in rights", proclaimed the French Declaration of Rights of 1789. Liberty and equality are the accepted twin pillars of democracy. Yet the civil engineering is complex: liberty and equality support democracy and reinforce each other; at the same time their contiguity causes strains in the edifice. Reinforcement occurs quite simply because the principle of freedom is not worth much if it is not equally enjoyed by all. On the other hand, freedom is· an individual issue, while equality is a social issue, and in some measure it is a matter of faith whether the two can coexist in complete harmony. The problem is soon stated. Freedom can undermine equality because people are not equally endowed with physical and intellectual powers and skills; free and untrammelled exercise of these powers and skills will consequently lead to inequality of economic and social position. Conversely, equality can undermine liberty since freedom to use one's gifts must be restrained for the sake of approximating to an egalitarian society. It is a dilemma which every democratic society must necessarily face.

Historically, freedom came first. The fight against the arbitrariness of the Star Chamber and on behalf of the freedoms of speech and religious belief was fought heroically in England in the seventeenth century by such notable figures as Coke, Milton and Locke. But equality did not enjoy a similar emphasis until the American and French revolutions of the following century.

But what is equality? The term cannot, clearly, be taken too literally. Rather does it imply that people should be treated without discrimination; should have equal opportunities to participate in their society. In political terms this means that all should have the right to vote and the right to enter political life. It was not until the nineteenth century that the franchise was effectively opened up to the mass of citizens. As the state impinged increasingly on people's lives, so demands grew for an effective say in government. [24] Nevertheless, the process was by no means completed by the time of the First World War, even in the most advanced democracies. Women acquired the vote later than men; in France not until 1945. Secondly, only very recently have we seen the age of majority reduced, in Britain and the USA, to eighteen. Most dramatic of all in recent years have been the Civil Rights movements, especially in the USA, where, although the Fifteenth Amendment forbade the withholding of the franchise from Negroes, millions of black people were in practice prevented from voting. The 1960s witnessed a massive campaign to rectify this situation.

However, Civil Rights are not solely a matter of political equality. Thus campaigns have been launched to achieve equitable schooling and desegregation in restaurants and buses for Negroes in the southern states of the USA, and better housing conditions for Roman Catholics in Northern Ireland. Equality, in short, has social and economic dimensions as well as specifically political. Of what use is the franchise, it is often argued, if economic inequality keeps bellies empty or the sick untended?

There are a wide range of ways in which economic equality can be promoted. The most widely accepted method is the welfare state technique whereby money is extracted by taxes from the wealthy in order to provide essential services for the less fortunate. Beyond this, there is the system of state control of industry in order to prevent the *private* accumulation of profits. [25] Thirdly, the most radical measure, is worker participation in the control of their industry, either by the use of consultative machinery or by full-blown syndicalism. [26] The fundamental question that must exercise the minds of economic egalitarians is the status of private property. Excessive inequalities of wealth are clearly not conducive to a democratic form of society. But is property, as Proudhon argued, no more than theft? Few would go as far as to propose utter propertyless uniformity. A marginal redistribution of wealth by taxation is the norm.

Economic equality presents many difficulties: social equality is a more popular and realistic aim. By taxation, legislation and the provision of free or cheap services like education it is possible to fudge the divisions between social classes, reduce the excessive privileges of the upper ranks of society, help the disadvantaged and enable people to forge their careers according to their talents rather than on the basis of influence and connections.

The major problem about the concept of equality when applied to the social and especially the economic sphere is to know where to stop. Having propounded the principle, there is no theoretical stopping point before complete uniformity. And yet pragmatically we know that this is probably neither practicable nor desirable. It would certainly not be democratic. A certain measure of inequality is built into human nature. Trade unionists strive to maintain wage differentials; middle-class housewives preen themselves because they own colour TV sets when their neighbours still gaze at black-and-white. Excess in either direction is intolerable; striking the right balance is incredibly difficult. "Inequality is easy," declared Tawney, "since it demands no more than to float with the current, equality is difficult for it involves swimming against it." [27]   Ultimately, what is essential, as W.G. Runciman has argued in *Relative Deprivation and Social Justice*, is to recognise that men are unequal in skills but to treat all with equal respect.

Democracy does not require either liberty or equality in undiluted forms, yet their complete absence would be fatal. It is all a matter of emphasis. Perhaps the central issue of emphasis concerns the relative weight to be accorded to each of these principles. For it is by attaching greater importance to equality than to freedom that one can approach the position of embracing one-party systems within the meaning of democracy. Allocation of the term democracy to a given regime is therefore likely to be dependent on the way a given observer balances the two qualities.

Participation

For all the classical importance of liberty and equality, the more recent rallying cry has been "participation". Utter the word and those in authority develop nervous ticks, signs of anger or schemes for revamping their machinery of government, depending on their position on the political spectrum; those who feel "left out" scent the coming of utopia. Demand for participation has been a widespread phenomenon in recent years. "In France 'participation' was one of the last of De Gaulle's rallying calls," records Carole Pateman; "in Britain we have seen the idea given official blessing in the Skeffington Report on planning, and in America the anti-poverty programme included a provision for the 'maximum feasible participation' of those concerned." [28]   And we might add to the list the Schools Action Union. The idea of participation was so in vogue in Britain in the late 1960s that a cabinet minister (Judith Hart) was even appointed in 1968 to be responsible for its development. It was a year later that the Skeffington Report, *People and Planning*, was published, recommending the involvement of the ordinary citizen in the processes of town planning and with obvious inferences for the extension of similar grass-roots participation in a variety of other fields. People are becoming more highly educated and politically conscious, especially through the medium of television, at the same time that government intervention in private lives is becoming increasingly pervasive.

Is increased participation desirable? There are two major caveats. One, expressed, for example, by Bernard Crick, [29] is that improved *communication* between government and governed is both more to be desired and more practical in a large modern state than any attempt to achieve total participation. The other is the belief that apathy is an essential ingredient for democracy. This belief is grounded in the assumption that the engagement of the great bulk of the populace in political activity would result in one of two unfortunate conditions: either inefficiency and instability; or the surrender of power to an authoritarian regime because the mass of the people do not want political responsibility. [30]

And yet, for all the debate, participation is nothing new — indeed it pre-dates civilisation itself. What we have witnessed in the past few years is, rather, a demand for a greater variety of ways for the individual to have a say in the way his life is run and for the established processes of representation and consultation to be used more efficiently. It is proposed to look at half-a-dozen major means of participation. These are: representation by parliamentary parties; referenda and plebiscites; the African one-party system; industrial democracy; and neighbourhood councils.

A representational system is a necessary concomitant of the size of the modern nation-state. Direct participation in the running of the state is possible only on the level of the Greek *polis*. The problem of the indirect, representational form of democracy is how to ensure that the elected representative truly reflects the views and interests of his constituents. One method clearly is to depute the representative to undertake quite specific tasks, to vote in certain ways on identified issues. The term "delegate" is usually reserved for a representative in this position. But it is far too cumbersome a piece of machinery to be used in a very widespread way. The normal method is to elect someone who will undertake to exercise his judgment about the best way to act and who will be held responsible for the manner in which he uses that judgment after the lapse of a given period of time following his election. Wherever there are national elected assemblies, whether democratic or not, this procedure is adopted. Indeed the system of representational parties antedates democracy, and their activities and policies have needed adjustment with the advent of mass democracy. Thus the citizen can participate indirectly in the government of his country by voting for and remaining in contact with his representative. However, there are many difficulties — hence the recent demands for other means of participation. Once elected, the MP in Britain, for example, has a variety of allegiances: he must serve to the best of his ability the interests of the country at large, he must support the policy of his party, and he must concern himself with the problems of his constituency as a whole, both those who voted for him and those who favoured other candidates. It is a difficult task. And it is made no easier when the simple majority as opposed to a proportional representation system is in operation. For example, hundreds of thousands of Liberal voters may feel that their views are only very partially represented in the House of Commons.

Elected representatives are intended as channels linking the government and the governed. It is sometimes felt that they act more like barriers. When this view prevails and a decision is needed on an issue of considerable national importance, some countries invoke the plebiscite or referendum. Britain's application to join the Common Market is a useful recent example of such an issue. M. Pompidou used a referendum on the question in France in 1972; Mr Wedgwood Benn, the archpriest of the cult of participation in Britain, has been a leading advocate of its employment in the United Kingdom. Superficially the plebiscite is an ideal tool for the direct involvement of the people in government decision-making. The people decide. But there are numerous snags. Who decides which issues are referendum-worthy? How does one ensure that the question is not ambiguous? More seriously, *shades* of opinion cannot be tested. Finally, and most serious of all, the plebiscite can be used by an unscrupulous political leader to enhance his own power by direct appeal to the people ("Bonapartism"), sidestepping the restraining authority of parliament or assembly.

As the age of British imperialism was drawing to its close the Mother of Parliaments felt it incumbent on her to spawn little ones over the globe. In some few places they survived, in others they became sickly. In Africa particularly they were often displaced by semi-indigenous step-children. The Anglo-Saxon two-party system is considered ill-fitted for most African states. Participation is achieved by other means. In Africa there is a much more urgent search for a Rousseauesque General Will than in Europe. And if the General Will is to rule there is no place for an opposition party. Unity of political effort and activity in most African states is both possible and necessary. It is possible because the political parties are frequently in effect nationalist movements formed to combat the imperial authority, now withdrawn, not another native party. In any case the foundation of most European party divisions lies in class conflict, and in Africa social divisions are drawn by tribe rather than by class. This, indeed, is the reason why African politicians set so much store by preventing the emergence of a multi-party system. If tribal divisions were hardened by party alignments there would be a very real danger that the country would disintegrate. Bloody communal clashes have already occurred in the Congo (now Zaïre), Nigeria, Uganda, Sudan, Rwanda and Burundi. The peril is all too manifest. Moreover, these countries need to sustain the momentum of the political effort that won them independence because of the severe economic problems with which they are confronted. In the words of the foremost exponent of the African system, Julius Nyerere: "To try and import the idea of a parliamentary opposition into Africa may very likely lead to violence — because the opposition parties will tend to be regarded as traitors by the majority of our people . . . trivial [party] manoeuvring. . . is an over-sophisticated pastime which we in Africa cannot afford to indulge in." [31] Also, the Africans place their faith in participatory activities of village and tribal consultative procedures to support their strivings towards democracy.

In Africa in many areas tribal elders and chieftains have consulted their people for countless ages; in Europe industrial managers are only just learning to consult with their workers. Industrial democracy is perhaps not as strictly political as some of the other systems we have examined here. But it is nearer to the hearts of most workmen, and, it is frequently argued, provides a firm — even necessary — foundation for political democracy; for, by participating in the affairs of their workplace, people become practised in the arts of democracy and more confident in their ability to play a participatory role generally. Advocates of industrial democracy therefore view it as the essential bedrock of an effective political democracy. The 1960s saw a revival of interest in the idea; a "revival" rather than the "beginning" because the theories of guild socialism and syndicalism were already forging the basic principles early in the century. Robert Kilroy-Silk has undertaken a very useful analysis of ideas about industrial democracy. [32] He distinguishes four different approaches. First, and probably the most influential in this country, is the idea of collective bargaining, which presupposes a considerable degree of trade union independence from state or managerial control. The importance of collective bargaining was underlined in the Labour Party's White Paper on industrial relations, *In*

Place of Strife:
  Collective bargaining [it states] is essentially a process by which employees take part in decisions that affect their working lives. If it is carried on by efficient management and representatives of well-organised unions, negotiating over a wide range of subjects, it represents the best method so far devised of advancing industrial democracy in the interests of both employees and employed. [33]

The second means of implementing industrial democracy is by workers' participation in management. Thirdly, there are schemes for co-ownership by workers, employers and investors. And most radical of all is the programme of the New Left for complete workers' control in the belief that capitalism and democracy are utterly incompatible. Some measure of cooperation between employers and employees has been achieved in Britain and France in recent years. The most notable developments have taken place in Yugoslavia, where the workers' self-management system, involving the management of all industrial enterprises of every type and size by Workers' Councils was first set up in 1950. Inevitably, the experiment has been the subject of much debate. Dr Pateman's conclusion is that "the Yugoslav experience gives us no good reason to suppose that the democratisation of industrial authority structure is impossible, difficult and complicated though it may be". [34]

The great size of the modern state is at one and the same time what makes participation both necessary and difficult. To circumvent the problem, manageable units must be identified: the factory is one, local geographical communities another. Established local authorities, whether county or borough, are too big to foster a sense of involvement among the bulk of the population. It is becoming increasingly recognised that if people are to participate in their own affairs with any conviction they must be involved in the concrete problems of their own home areas. Thus the neighbourhood council movement has got under way in a number of English cities — councils to perform the functions of social service and consultation. There are several problems inherent in the system. To be effective the areas must be small, probably no more than 10,000 inhabitants. And if they are to achieve anything they must be active without clashing too violently with the established local authority, and be duly elected without being swallowed by the party machine. In the late 1960s a number of *ad hoc* councils evolved. By 1970 the movement had sufficiently caught on for the Association of

Neighbourhood Councils to be established. Then, in the following year, the most famous of these councils came into being: with financial aid from the Rowntree Trust proper elections were held for the launching of the neighbourhood council for the Golborne Area of Notting Hill. The era of participatory self-help had opened. Both Pericles and Samuel Smiles would be content.

Democracy today

Democracy is now a "hurrah" word: it is a form of government which today is almost uniformly favoured in principle: the Second World War was said to be a struggle fought in its defence; in 1948 the United Nations adopted the Universal Declaration of Human Rights which contains a number of democratic principles. We live in an age of democratic pretensions. But how widespread is the actuality?

To answer this question we are thrown back to Professor Macpherson's threefold definition. Are the liberal-democratic states of the West to reserve the title to themselves or have the one-party states of the Communist system and Africa a different but none the less just as valid a claim? The issue centres on the relative importance of the concepts of equality and liberty. Historically, the states of the Western world achieved political liberty before they attempted to achieve any measure of equality, and even so it took them a considerable time to evolve a truly democratic system. The Communist and African countries have started on the road much later and have moved off from a different starting-point giving priority to equality rather than liberty. However, if one has to choose between liberty and equality, is not liberty to be preferred? With liberty established, effective political dialogue can be undertaken and change can be brought about through the clash of opinion. Policies leading to greater equality can be adopted. The important point is that options are open. This is true democracy. We must therefore ask whether there is sufficient freedom in one-party states to make the use of the term democracy at all realistic. Macpherson lays down three conditions concerning the democratic operation of the party itself, which he feels need to be satisfied if one-party states are to be considered fully democratic. He is forced to conclude that "It does not appear that these three conditions have as yet been met in any communist states" though the claim of the African states "is I think somewhat better than that of the communist states . . . [because] there has generally been no need of a class state after the revolution". [35]

It is more profitable, though less tidy, to speak in terms of movement towards democracy or of democratic elements in a government than to make a clearcut distinction between democratic and non-democratic regimes. [36] On this basis, the liberal-democratic regimes of the West have travelled farther, are closer to the ideal (whatever that may be). Throughout the world pro-democratic and anti-democratic forces coexist in the same societies — not, it is true, nearly so clearly demarcated as in the 1930s, but nevertheless the tension is there. The steady development of the facilities of education and mass communication is strengthening the political consciousness of hundreds of millions of people, who in consequence press for some measure of participation in the governmental process. At the same time government is becoming such a complex business that bureaucratisation is draining democracy of its credibility. In the last resort it is will-power and confidence in the crucial human importance of democracy that will tell. It was precisely these qualities that advanced the democratic cause in the North Atlantic area in the last century. We cannot afford to be complacent now.

5 Organisation of the Political Unit

The problem of identification

Robinson Crusoe's elation at discovering Man Friday; the mind-warping horrors of solitary confinement; the sensation of organic unity in a crowd of football team supporters; the nagging wretchedness of being sent to Coventry: these varied human experiences bear indisputable testimony to the very basic psychological need of mankind, the need to relate with one's fellows; the need to associate with others; ultimately, the need to identify with a group. Man is not by nature an isolate. Saints or cranks pursue the eremitical life; it is not the norm. And so sacred is the bond that ties a people together that it is often ritualised in the most solemn manner in both primitive and sophisticated societies: by awful initiation into the tribe and by utter dedication to the national flag.

Identification is, however, a dual process, for if the members of a society are bonded together by a powerful sense of community, they are, by the same token, differentiated from non-members. The intrusion of non-members is often guarded against, either out of a sense of fear or of superiority: in the Valley of the Blind the behaviour of the sighted man was strange, so he was to be blinded, and he fled in terror to the safety of the hills.

Village, city-state, tribe and empire have all served as the unit of identification. The nation-state was invented in Europe in comparatively modern times, its ideology, nationalism, shaped largely by German philosophers of the early nineteenth century: Herder, Fichte, Jahn. It was Pastor Schleiermacher who summed up the individual's absorption in the nation in the following words:

How little worthy of respect is the man who roams about hither and thither without the anchor of national ideal and love of fatherland; ... how the greatest source of pride is lost by the woman that cannot feel that she also bore children for her fatherland... that her house and all the petty things that fill up most of her time belong to a greater whole and take their place in the union of her people. [1]

Nationalism is now a universal fact of political life, the most vigorous and pervasive of all political creeds. Indeed, nationalism is so entrenched in modern man's political thinking that a conscious effort must be made to remind oneself that there is nothing especially "natural" or "inevitable" about the nation-state as an institution or nationalism as an idea: rather did they emerge as responses to particular historical circumstances. There were states long before nationalism existed; and even today there are many multi-national states — including the United Kingdom. Thus, although the bulk of this chapter is devoted to an analysis of nationalism by virtue of its current force and significance, we must also recognise the existence of nascent alternative ideas, complementary to each other but corrosive of obsessional nationalism; these are the ideas of provincialism and supranationalism, emphasising respectively loyalty to one's local region and the essential oneness of the human race.

The origins and strength of nationalism

The powerful appeal of nationalism clearly demands an explanation. And since the appeal of a doctrine is but an alternative way of stating that the doctrine has been the response to a social need, an examination of the origins of nationalism must feature in this explanation. However, before we square up to the issue of the peculiar power of nationalism, we must define with some precision what we understand by the term.

Precision is difficult when the root word "nation" is popularly used so loosely. Devotees of Hollywood Westerns will think of the Iroquois nation, a tribal connotation; students of international affairs will respond with the term United Nations Organisation in which the term clearly denotes a sovereign political unit; while mellifluous Welshmen singing at the national Eisteddfod assume a cultural meaning. We may put it quite simply, if not very helpfully, that a nation is a group of people who feel a sense of community, feel that they have a right to stand free and together as an identifiable component of mankind. This drawing together may be the result of social moulding by any one or more centripetal forces such as a common language, shared traditions, religious identification or occupation of a clearly defined geographical receptacle. The essence of nationalism is the insistence that such a coherent cultural group should be geographically coterminous with a political unit: the frontiers of the political "nation" should coincide with the fringes of the cultural "nation". If this coincidence does not obtain, then the nationalist will seek to effect changes to bring it about, by securing independence from foreign political control, by unifying his scattered people and by the assertion of a self-conscious national pride.

In a sense the bulk of this chapter is an attempt to define nationalism. The above paragraph is, therefore, only an initial framework, the individual features of which will be delineated in more detail later on. Just two more introductory notes. First, nationalism is not synonymous with xenophobia — hatred of the foreigner. You can be a nationalist and respect the individuality of other nations; at least, people like Mazzini have thought so. Nor is nationalism synonymous with patriotism — love of your country. Your country may not be a nation-state. The Soviet Union, for example, is a great patchwork of nations in the cultural sense, a fact clearly recognised by Stalin when he declared the struggle against Nazi Germany "the Great Patriotic War" in order to mobilise unified support by the many nations for the country as a whole. In the second place, it must be noted that nationalism as defined here is closely bound up not just with popular self-consciousness but with a belief in popular sovereignty — that the mass of the people have a right to determine their own destinies. Such ideas emerged, in Europe, only in the late eighteenth century. To stretch the term to embrace the more amorphous sense of nationality associated, for example, with the France of Joan of Arc or the England of Elizabeth I is to make it a shapeless intellectual garment, a voluminous sweater that envelops rather than emphasises the salient points of interest.

Nationalism originated as an ideological response to certain social conditions and needs in Europe in the late eighteenth century. It was exported together with other European merchandise, such as Christianity and cheap textiles, from the metropolitan countries to their Asian and African colonies, where, by the mid-twentieth century, social conditions obtained parallel to those in eighteenth-century Europe. What were these conditions that favoured the evolution of nationalism? Put briefly, it was the collapse of the traditional frames of identity. Before the age of nationalism group identification for the masses of the population meant allegiance to the village community. The village community was compact because it was so immobile: inhabitants rarely left the village, outsiders rarely came in. Thomas Hardy's reddleman was more fascinating as a contact with the "outside world" than for his bizarre appearance. Horizons were tightly constrained: the Russian word *mir* means both "commune" and "world"; for the Russian peasant's village *was* his world. Paradoxically, while the peasant's sense of identity was parochial, the intellectual's was cosmopolitan. The humane men of letters of the Enlightenment took the world as their parish; while the professional men of the Ivory Coast or Nigeria thought of themselves as members of the wide flung French and British empires.

By the turn of the eighteenth century in Europe and by the mid-twentieth century in the Afro-Asian countries these two bonds of loyalty had snapped simultaneously so that both the general mass of people and the middle class were searching for new identities. By expanding their vision, the masses could identify with the nation-state; the same identification was achieved by the middle class by contracting their focus. And it is perhaps this coincidence of identity that has given the resultant nationalism such power.

The collapse of old loyalties needs explanation. The village community was destroyed by the processes of industrialisation and urbanisation. The crust of immobility was broken as labour migrated to the towns. For these people, uprooted from their village and tribal communities, nationalism filled a psychological void. [2] It is more difficult to generalise about the collapse of middle-class cosmopolitanism. It had always been much frailer, of course, than the village attachment of the peasant. The delicate bloom of eighteenth-century cosmopolitanism was crushed underfoot by the brutal realities of the Revolutionary and Napoleonic wars. As for the middle class in the colonies of Asia and Africa, they became disenchanted with the imperial regimes, which they had viewed initially as magnificent modernising forces but which they came increasingly to see as instruments of exploitation by the white man. The wog — the Westernised Oriental Gentleman — was suspended in a tantalising limbo, educated out of his own society and at the same time not fully accepted by the white man's.

Nationalism originated in Europe and much of its momentum there has been sustained. Hitler capitalised on the tradition of 1848 and Bismarck, de Gaulle on the Napoleons; while Nagy, embattled in Budapest in 1956, appealed to the memory of Kossuth. However, the main, dramatic strength of nationalism in most recent times has lain in the Afro-Asian world. The beginnings of Afro-Asian nationalism therefore needs a special word. Nationalist movements had already started, notably in India, by the late nineteenth century. A great fillip was given to these organisations by three wars: the Russo-Japanese war showed that an Asiatic country could defeat a European power, while the mobilisation of colonial troops by the Allies in the two world wars made large numbers of African and Asian men politically conscious for the first time. The watershed was 1947. Progress before that year had been of prehistoric slowness; then in 1947, Britain conceded independence to the Indian subcontinent, the most vast colonial dependency in the world. A truly watershed year, for, in the fifteen years that followed, a veritable cascade of colonies became independent. The speed and extent of the process far exceeded any visions that anyone could have had in 1947. Once the flow had started it could not be stemmed, except in southern Africa.

And what of Britain? Britain has displayed her share of that form of nationalism which expresses itself as a self-assertive, aggressive pride — witness the Suez episode of 1956. However, the greatest interest has focused on the so-called Celtic fringe of Ireland, Scotland and Wales. The Irish people have a long history of resentment towards English domination. It is scarcely surprising, therefore, that in the nineteenth century, when the Poles were demanding independence from Russia and the Hungarians from Austria, a fully fledged nationalist movement should evolve in Ireland. Nevertheless, when the principle of Home Rule was conceded, the Protestant segment in Ulster suddenly became fearful of their possible future subjection as a minority group. Hence the partition. Irish nationalism persists in the Sinn Fein party and its military wing, the IRA, who continue to campaign for the reunification of the island. In comparison, the movements in Wales and Scotland are less prone to violence: the complaint that "the value of Scottish whisky in bond exceeds the total gold reserves in the Bank of England" [3] is not the spirit that inspires the IRA urban guerrillas in Ulster. The Welsh and Scottish movements are also more youthful, Plaid Cymru and the Scottish National Party originating only in the 1920s and developing the slight political weight they have only as recently as the 1960s when it was felt that the major British parties were giving insufficient attention to the economic problems of these two countries. National *political* consciousness is, as will be shown below, inextricably bound up with national *cultural* consciousness. Pride in a common Celtic heritage has fluttered through Britain's fringe to meet a resonant ripple from Brittany — the French fringe. These trimmings of the ancient Celtic people have even claimed places in the United Nations Organisation.

Although we have examined the origins and persistence of nationalism as a political force, the strength of the ideology needs some further explanation. It has already been suggested that its twin appeal to both the masses and the middle classes is an important characteristic in this respect. [4] Let us dwell a while longer on the middle-class element. For the neglected truth is that nationalism is not a spontaneous popular phenomenon. The masses are indeed mobilised to exert pressure, but the initiative comes from the middle-class professional layer of society. It is the lawyers, doctors, teachers, civil servants and army officers who organise the nationalist movements; some, like Gandhi, motivated by selfless idealism, the majority by sheer professional frustration because, educated to conform to a competitive society, they find their ways to senior posts barred by an aristocratic or, worse, a foreign élite. It is this boiling frustration, particularly in the Afro-Asian world, that has provided the nationalist ideology with its potent head of steam. The resentment was vividly expressed in India as early as 1881 by Dadabhai Naoroji:

The thousands that are being sent out by the universities every year find themselves in an anomalous position. There is no place for them in their motherland. They may beg in the streets or break stones on the roads, for aught the rulers seem to care for their national rights, position and duties in their own country. [5]

The aims of nationalism

Like the Magi of old, nationalists are bearers of three gifts: the gold of freedom, the frankincense of unity and the myrrh of pride.

The terms "nationalism" and "independence" are often used almost synonymously. This is confusing. Independence can be achieved without the force of nationalism, while nationalism can have aims quite different from, indeed sometimes, with reluctant provinces, antipathetic to, independence. The confusion is, in fact, the understandable result of the dramatic emergence of so many colonial territories to independent statehood under the motive force of nationalist ideologies in recent years: 800 million people in the years 1945–60. The nature of the relationship between nationalism and independence is therefore of considerable importance if the phenomenon in its modern aspect is to be fully understood. For an independence movement to be nationalist it must be suffused with a consciousness of a cultural identity which at one and the same time binds together the rebellious people and sets them apart from their political masters. Thus the American War of Independence, prominent landmark though it was in the history of freedom movements, was not nationalist in tone. The desire for truly national freedom can in fact assume three forms: the creation of a brand new state; the replacement of a foreign by an indigenous government involving no change of boundaries; and the secession of a minority people from the main block of the state.

The genesis of a completely new state is a rare occurrence. One might classify the creation of Pakistan in 1947 as such an event. However, the persistence of political instability in Pakistan, crescendoing to the massive human tragedy that accompanied the tearing away of Bangladesh from the control of Islamabad, is sad evidence of the artificiality of a state whose very name is an artifact. Continuous tension with India further darkens the picture. This is not to apportion blame; rather to suggest that the creation of a new state can occasion the most intractable problems. Nor, again suspending judgment, has the history of Israel, the example *par excellence* of the creation of a new state, been any more felicitous. Embedded in an area of the world overwhelmingly Arab in composition, stretching over land inhabited for centuries by Arabs, the state of Israel could hardly fail to provoke the bitterest Arab resentment by its very existence. The coincidence in time and place of Israel and Arab nationalism has been tragic. At the beginning of the century Israel was a nation without a state, while the Arab countries were formed into states without a sense of nationality. But Zionism resolved the Israeli dilemma just as Arab nationalism burgeoned. Nevertheless, it is true that Czechoslovakia and Yugoslavia, creations of the postwar settlement of 1919, have enjoyed happier even if not entirely uneventful histories – evidence that new nation-states can be successfully forged.

The sombre history of the world since 1945 has been enlivened on scores of occasions by the cheerful raucousness of independence celebrations as colonies — former dependencies of the British, French and Dutch — have achieved their sovereign status in the world. The vast red, green and orange slabs of colour on the map have melted into a complex mosaic of nation-states. Imperialism has retreated before nationalism; sometimes in bloody anger, sometimes in gracious friendship, on occasion leaving neglectful anarchy.

The goal of independence was enshrined in nationalist terms in the principle of national self-determination by Woodrow Wilson as the bedrock of the Versailles settlement and of a peaceful world hereafter. The idea was made flesh in Asia by the independence of India in 1947 and in Africa of Ghana a decade later. Expectations of freedom became universal and in much of colonial Asia and Africa nationalist movements became irresistible forces. Where they met immovable obstacles explosions occurred: hence the guerrilla war mounted by Frelimo in Mozambique, the Mau Mau crisis in Kenya, and, most vicious of all, the seven-year-long struggle of the Front de Libération Nationale (FLN) in Algeria. In the weary years of war in Algeria tempers became frayed: acts of urban terrorism by the Muslims were countered by the widespread use of brutal torture by the French security forces. Finally, France stood discredited in the eyes of the world; Algerian nationalism emerged triumphant and heroic. Indeed, in the view of the apostle of the Algerian revolt, Frantz Fanon, the very use of violence was necessary to cleanse the wretched of the earth and endow them with a proper pride in their own identity and worth. As Sartre has explained, "to shoot down a European is to kill two birds with one stone, to destroy an oppressor and the man he oppresses at the same time: there remain a dead man, and a free man; the survivor, for the first time, feels a *national* soil under his feet. At this moment the nation . . . is one with his liberty." [6] Although the great majority of national liberation movements in recent years have operated in Asia and Africa, one must not forget the attempts by East European states to secure greater freedom from Soviet control, notably by Hungary and Czechoslovakia. Despite the compression of events into a few days, considerable violence attended the essentially nationalist uprising of the Hungarian people in the autumn of 1956.

Serious exceptions like Algeria aside, the process of decolonisation since 1945 has been remarkably peaceful. It is true that imperial governments have been hesitant and that there have been riots and political imprisonments (it is a rather weak joke that no one can become the leader of an ex-British colony unless he has been in gaol). But on the whole, very little violence was necessary to persuade the British and French to withdraw from Africa or the Dutch from the East Indies. The wind of change was tempered by the calm of negotiated handover, often involving an easy transition period extending across the independence date as European administrators have been steadily replaced by native personnel.

A transition period has been important since violence may accompany independence — not between imperial power and colony, but within the colony — if the new government has not the prepared strength and stability to sustain an efficient administration. The act of independence cost hundreds of thousands of lives in both India and the Belgian Congo because communal forces were unleashed that were too powerful for the new governments to contain. The situation in India was extremely complex and it is difficult to judge whether the British government could or should have acted differently. In the Congo, however, the Belgians had simply taken no steps to prepare the huge country for self-government. Served by a pathetically skeletal band of skilled personnel, socially rent by re-emergent tribal rivalries, politically torn by faction fights, confusion worse confounded by the machinations of outside powers greedy for the mineral riches of the Katanga province: such were the ingredients of the Congo anarchy of 1960. It is sometimes better to hasten slowly.

The nationalism of the two decades following the Second World War was characterised by established, if subordinate, political units gaining independence. But independence can also be achieved by fragments seceding from a larger block. The incidence and vigour of this kind of movement has been noticeably increasing in recent years. It is useful in this instance to provide a list of the main examples to show how widespread the phenomenon is. The British Isles itself provides interesting examples: Eire has already achieved its independence; the Welsh and Scots seek more autonomy. In Europe highly organised and vociferous nationalist movements seek at least greater autonomy and consideration from their governments: for the Bretons in France, the Basques in Spain, the Flemings in Belgium and Croatians in Yugoslavia. In the Afro-Asian world, the Kurds in Iraq and the Nagas in India have fought especially stubborn guerrilla wars in their hills for many years;

while the unsuccessful attempt by the Ibos to set up a state of Biafra independent of Nigeria and the successful establishment of Bangladesh by the East Bengalis have been played out quite recently as dramas of epic proportions and quality. Even the New World has been infected by this fever of mini-nationalism. In the USA some of the most militant among the Negroes, believing that no amount of ameliorative reform can bridge the gap between black and white, seriously seek the partition of the country and the formation of a separate Negro state. [7] Finally, in Canada, a forceful movement among the francophone population demands the secession of Quebec.

The Québecois movement made dramatic headlines when in 1970 it kidnapped and held to ransom two important officials. Terrorism by explosions, shooting and kidnapping, besides the use of mass demonstrations to draw attention to their demands − these are familiar and obvious, if ignoble, devices used by a movement to achieve an impact out of all proportion to its numerical strength. It is sometimes suggested that the threatened partition of established states by means of these tactics represents a "new" nationalism, but neither the use of violence nor the small size of the proposed units are new features of nationalism. Indeed, the size of a nation is not a relevant issue to the nationalist. He would argue that any people who feel themselves to be a coherent unit should be considered a nation and should form a nation-state. The logic of the nationalist case requires that the world should be continually carved up into separate states until all these desires are satisfied (or sublimated). What probably is new in these provincial movements is the reaction against the centralising power of the modern state: there is widespread resentment at the homogenisation of provincial characteristics, which expresses itself where it can in nationalistic form. [8]

If a nation is under foreign domination (however perceived), nationalism expresses itself as a demand for freedom; if the nation is scattered in a number of different states, nationalism comes as a unifier. This raises the basic question, already briefly alluded to, [9] namely, what characterises a nation? Precisely which pieces make up the complete jigsaw? Natural frontiers, such as mountain ranges? But so frequently there are no obvious physical boundaries; even where there are, migrations of peoples often make them meaningless. What about religion, then? This is a rare indicator, important usually when it highlights the differences between neighbours (for example, Ireland *v.*

England, Pakistan *v.* India). Language has been most frequently represented as the true key to nationality, from the German nationalist in Napoleonic times who considered that any girl who learnt French was delivering herself up to prostitution, to the Welsh educationalists of today who struggle to retain the teaching of the tongue as the means of sustaining a sense of Welshness. There is good sense here: to achieve a feeling of identity one must express it in language. And yet, again, the world is too complex for this test to operate universally: English, Spanish and French are spoken by a great range of nations, while many an Asian and African nation-state contains within itself a veritable babel of languages. We come finally to the most intangible and at the same time the most real of all the tests: a sense of common tradition and experience. A people is a nation when it is conscious of a common culture enjoyed, common struggles endured. A nation is a nation. Nationalism is historical consciousness. [10]

By such magnetic forces are people drawn together. The process of unification operates in three major ways. First, in the classical pattern laid down by nineteenth-century Italy and Germany, there is the fusion of two or more separate states. Thus did the present state of Somalia come into being, composed of the former British and Italian colonies. Somalia also provides a useful example of the second expression of the trend towards unification – irredentism. [11] Somali people live in border provinces of the neighbouring countries of Ethiopia and Kenya: Somali nationalists believe that these provinces should be incorporated into Somalia. Similarly, Spain claims that Gibraltar should revert to Spanish control, the Enosis movement believes that Cyprus should become part of Greece, Austria and Italy haggle over possession of the Tyrol, while the Sinn Fein and the IRA aim to redeem Ulster for the Irish nation. Irredentism is the adjustment of boundaries considered by nationalists to be unfairly drawn; a tidying-up operation involving comparatively small areas.

At the other extreme are the massive pan-movements. These are movements that accord a very generous, wide-ranging definition to their respective nations. For example, Pan-Arabism seeks to unite into a single state all Arab people of north Africa and the Middle East from the Straits of Gibraltar to the Persian Gulf. Likewise, Pan-Africanism seeks to give political expression to what it considers to be the essential oneness of black, sub-Saharan Africa. Numerous Arab and African leaders, notably Nasser and Nkrumah, while building up the independence and self-pride of their own states, preached the gospel of the wider unity. Nkrumah urged a "unity which is a prerequisite of true independence. . . . I mean to an African Continental government — *a single Continent* which would develop a feeling of one community among the peoples of Africa." [12] And numerous attempts have been made to endow the ideas with reality. One technique is the step-by-step construction of limited regional federations. Egypt, renaming itself the United Arab Republic, has been the centre of several of these attempts, the most recent experiment linking it with Libya and Syria. This method has met with little success. Nor has the alternative — subcontinental unity by a single bound — had a happier history. Both the Arab League and the Organisation of African Unity have been fraught with dissension.

The third gift of nationalism is pride, a portmanteau word containing a jumble of emotions including a sympathetic understanding of the nation's past achievements, a neighbourly feeling of loyalty towards one's fellow citizens, a nervous anxiety that the nation should be highly regarded in the world, a fierce defence of the nation's territory and rights, and an aggressive hostility towards other nations who might seem to be undermining the integrity or dignity of one's own nation. This brew of emotions is usually brought to the boil by nationalist leaders for one of two reasons, either as an adhesive to cement together a loosely grouped collection of people or as a balm to salve a pride hurt by some international humiliation. Dr Sukarno skilfully manipulated the confrontation with Malaysia and the irredentist claim on West Irian to infuse some sense of community into his 3000-island Muslim — Christian — Communist republic of Indonesia. In the second category one may cite the antics of General de Gaulle — needling Churchill during the Second World War, insisting on an independent *force de frappe* during the Cold War, humiliating Macmillan by vetoing Britain's first application to join the Common Market, all to prove that France was still a force to be reckoned with despite the humiliations of Nazi occupation, governmental instability under the Fourth Republic and the military defeat in Indo-China. This emphasis on national pride can, of course, lash out in an aggressive show of force. Hitler's policies were particularly degenerate examples of this condition. But on a much more moderate scale Britain was guilty of what was essentially a similar reaction in the Suez episode of 1956.

Some people would dub Britain's action against Nasser, righteous indignation. It depends on your point of view. Nationalism has tended to take the form of righteous indignation in the British Isles in recent years. The depressed condition of Catholics in Ulster has been explained with some bitterness as follows: "In Northern Ireland Catholics are Blacks who happen to have white skins. . . . The Northern Ireland problem is a colonial problem." [13] While the handling of Scottish affairs at Westminster has been described as "an incredible record of insult, arrogance, ill-faith, unscrupulousness, ignorance and indifference, that can have few if any parallels in the relationships of any two nations in the so-called civilized world" [14]

The paradoxes of nationalism

The practical aims of nationalism, though a little complex because of the varying circumstances in which it operates, are fairly clear. When, however, we examine the political style of the nationalist a number of paradoxes appear.

Firstly, one may ask, is nationalism a force for international peace or conflict? In view of what has been said above about aggressive nationalist pride, the obvious response would seem to be "conflict". Indeed, the history of the past one and a half centuries is strewn with wars readily labelled by the historians as nationalist. Claims to independence and irredentist issues have proved fertile grounds for conflict. Nationalist pride has, moreover, been a powerful cause of imperialist expansion — a serious source of conflict in the modern world. Yet one must not cast aside too hastily the peaceful potential of nationalism. Many supporters of the doctrine, notably Mazzini and President Wilson, besides the Afro-Asian exponents more recently, have argued that conflict has been caused by the *frustration* of national self-determination rather than its free play and that peace and stability can be expected in the world only when the nationalist's ideal of a patchwork of properly defined nation-states has been achieved. "Every people", Mazzini wrote, "is bound to constitute itself a nation before it can occupy itself with the question of humanity." [15] The ambivalence is built into the theory.

There is ambivalence, too, in the internal approach to politics adopted by the nationalist. A liberal, democratic relationship would seem a logical extension of the principle of national self-determination. After all, if the people of a nation claim independence as a right in order to determine their own destinies, it might appear somewhat contradictory to surrender freedom of political action to a dictatorial government after independence. Indeed, historically the concepts of nationalism and popular sovereignty emerged together in the era of the French Revolution. More recently it was the touchstone of the nationalism of Gandhi and Nehru: Indian democracy is part of her proud nationalist tradition. The search, especially in Tanzania, for a specially African form of democracy and socialism might be interpreted as belonging basically to the same tradition. [16] However, nationalism is heavily dependent upon symbolism; and there is nothing more powerfully symbolic than a mighty father-figure. Unfortunately, the great leader of his people can so easily degenerate into a power-hungry dictator. The cult of Nkrumah was a perfect example, complete with statues in public places, a sycophantic youth movement, the imprisonment of opponents and the majestic title of "The Redeemer". What is more, the nationalist process of exalting the nation to a position where it is conceived of as virtually a living organism in its own right with an existence independent of the individuals of which it is composed leads logically to the subordination of the interests of the individual to the nation, indeed if necessary the sacrifice of the individual for the state. [17]

With the final paradox of nationalism we reach the heart of the doctrine: this is its Janus-like attitude towards history and progress. Just as an amnesiac loses his sense of identity, so a nation without a collective memory — a conscious history — is a society lacking a proper identity. Hence the heavy emphasis on past glories by nations with established histories and the frantic search for historical roots by nations whose past self-knowledge is of limited scope. This emphasis on historical tradition expresses itself in a number of ways. Sometimes it is no more than the renaming of a state — such as Mali and Ghana to recall the grandeur of past West African civilisations, or Alba (Scotland) and Cymru (Wales) to emphasise the past linguistic identity of these people. Emphasis on linguistic identity, expressed through a nationally conscious literature, is also a device, noticeable in the Scottish and Welsh movements, for example, to sustain links with an identifiable culture of the past. Memories of past events are kept alive by celebrations: the Orangeist phenomenon of Northern Ireland reeks with the history of the war with James II in 1689, while the persistence of the rite of clitorectomy among the Mau Mau represented a clinging to the past against the erosions of Europeanisation. The connection between present and past emphasised by nationalists is sometimes quite phoney, for the simple reason that the history of many of these societies is discontinuous. For Greeks in the 1820s, Italians in the 1930s, Egyptians in the 1950s, Ghanaians also in the 1950s to bathe in the reflected glories of the great civilisations of many centuries before just because they happen to bear the name or occupy the same territory is little more than a confidence trick, the implication being that the qualities that produced these civilisations are latent still in the modern nations. It is all part of the morale-boosting exercise, but it cannot stand up to reasoned examination. Perhaps the most notorious of these spurious appeals to history in recent years has been the assertion by Ghanaians, in pictorial form, that it was Africans who taught the alphabet and mathematics to the Greeks, originated the sciences of chemistry and medicine, even invented shorthand!

Nevertheless, for all this immersion in history, nationalists are marked by a desire, almost an obsession, to modernise their states. In the Afro-Asian world, of course, it is part of the desperate anxiety to improve standards of living. Hydroelectric and irrigation dams in Egypt, Ghana and India have become almost symbols of national grandeur. But the desire to keep up with the Joneses is not confined to the Third World. If for "Volta Dam" one reads "Concorde", one sees that the same forces operate in Britain. The urge for modernisation is not, however, just a matter of competitiveness – an international gap; rather is it a gap between complacent age and importunate youth. Perhaps the nationalists invented the generation gap? For what is the most common adjective adopted by nationalist movement? "Young": Young Italy, Young Ireland, the Young Turks, Young Arabism – and the examples could be multiplied. This desire by the nationalist to renovate his society is related, of course, to the professional frustration of the middle classes already noted. Nationalism is social dynamism.

The fallacy of nationalism
Nationalism is a complex doctrine shot through with contradictions. However, theoretical consistency is not the only test. We must ask whether nationalism enhances human social efficiency and happiness? To be fair to the reader I must show my hand. I believe the development of nationalism to have been a misfortune. This is not to deny the beneficial effects of independence and modernisation; rather to object to their realisation in a national context. In the first place,

nationalism is not a useful doctrine. It does not enhance human welfare because it places the interest of the nation above the happiness of the individual and runs counter to the regional and global trends of the modern economy and technology. Secondly, nationalism is a doctrine that inflames the emotions and therefore encourages fanatical commitment rather than the will to compromise and to fit together the best from different elements which is the essence of civilised political behaviour. Finally, the basic tenet of nationalism, that the political unit should coincide with the cultural, leads to undesirable actions such as the break-up of economically viable units (as with the threatened break-up of Nigeria or as would happen in the United Kingdom if the Scottish nationalists had their way), or the inhumane transfer of great communities of people (for example, the expulsion of the Germans from the Oder-Neisse lands of Poland after the Second World War). The fact of the matter is, the nationalist ideal is impossible. For all practical purposes a state must occupy a compact geographical area. Nations, in the cultural sense (however identified) are not distributed over the face of the earth in neat packages. Within the British Isles, the Irish decide they should have a separate political existence; in Ireland the Ulstermen decide they should be separate from the rest of the island; in Ulster the Catholic portions of Londonderry and Belfast dislike being part of a predominantly Protestant Ulster: boxes within boxes within boxes . . . No cartographer, however ingenious, can draw boundaries to meet all these demands. Lord Acton perceived this clearly. He wrote:

> A State which is incompetent to satisfy different races condemns itself; a State which labours to neutralise, to abort, or to expel them, destroys its own vitality; a State which does not include them is destitute of the chief basis of self-government. The theory of nationality, therefore, is a retrograde step. [18]

The problem is to wean mankind away from the nationalism that has provided his psychological nourishment in recent years to an intellectual and emotional diet better suited to his present sophisticated social condition.

Provincialism [19]

A man living in Kiev may think of himself as a Ukrainian rather than a Russian; a man in Aix, a Provençal; a man in Kumasi, an Ashanti. These hypothetical people need not be nationalists in the sense of wanting to secede from the state of which they are citizens: they might just have a sense of loyalty to their own particular province. Such a province, it is true, may be an incipient nation: it depends on the strength of the feeling, which may express itself in the violence of Basque terrorism or merely in the bitterness of the opposing supporters in the Roses cricket match. When does loyalty to a province become a desire for nationalist secession? It is rather like trying to demarcate where the red band ends and the orange begins in a rainbow. We have already seen [20] that the bonds of loyalty to the established nation-state are loosening in many countries of the world. Existent states are seen as merely the successful artifacts of history and the nationalists in their dissident provinces now wish to succeed in their bid to create new states. However, complete independence is only the most extreme form of a more generalised desire to weaken centralised political control.

Local or provincial loyalty may have quite deep historical roots. Many states today are amalgamations of territories that have had independent political or cultural existence in the past. This loyalty may, as with the Frenchman's identity with his *petite patrie*, enjoy no effective institutional expression. In other countries, recognition of former autonomy is afforded by a federal constitution, as in West Germany and Yugoslavia, for example.

The main purpose of a federal as opposed to a unitary constitution is to diffuse power, to prevent the concentration of too much control in the hands of the central government. This is the aim of those who today demand greater provincial autonomy, though there are two sides to the devolutionary coin: for some the main goal is greater administrative efficency; for others it is greater, more democratic, political control. The change of emphasis from vertical departmental control to horizontal provincial control has been a common feature of economic administration in a number of industrial countries in recent years. In 1957 Khrushchev caused considerable comment by the industrial reorganisation involved in the creation of the regional *sovnarkhoses*. In 1964 came the appointment of regional prefects and Regional Economic Development Committees (CODERs) in France. Britain followed suit with the establishment of Economic Planning Regions, while the division of the country into a number of provincial regions has been an important feature of recent schemes for local government reorganisation, including the important Maud Report (1969). Such reforms are merely a recognition of a simple fact that different areas have different needs, problems and resources and that central planners are too remote to take these fully into consideration.

Administrative devolution, however, only goes halfway towards meeting the demands for decentralisation; and exponents of provincial autonomy, like the Scottish and Welsh nationalists, for example, are not satisfied with such partial measures. The basic point at issue, expressed in a number of other current protest movements like the New Left, is the "facelessness" and remoteness of government. Involvement, effective participation in decision-making procedures, is what the provincial movement is really all about. The establishment of provincial authorities with powers of some weight would, it is believed, provide for more meaningful individual participation in government and a counterbalance to the central government. In Britain it has been admitted that "there must be a fundamental change in the attitude to local government of the national authorities. The national Government must give local authorities a larger measure of home rule";[21] though it is recognised that "the idea of division of powers and that the government's writ might not run throughout the country on all issues is really foreign to much political thinking in Britain."[22]

There would seem to be a major distinction between the programmes of the full-blooded nationalist and the proponent of provincial autonomy: the nationalist requires complete sovereignty for his territory; the provincial wishes for a sharing of power. Yet the distinction is not a fast one. Even the first Welsh Nationalist MP has admitted that "what nationalists seek is, not separation from England, but a different kind of link — a handshake rather than a handcuff".[23]
However, the model of relationships that is emerging in some people's minds [24] requires a round of handshakes that would overwhelm an octopus. The idea is that the number of political units should multiply considerably but that they should coexist in pyramidal form — local, provincial, national, regional, even global. Links between the tiers should be facilitated, and so the kind of boundaries that currently exist between nation-states must be reduced in strength. The nation-state must be reduced from its present pre-eminent position to being just one of the layers, the attack on its sovereignty being made from two fronts: one is the strengthening of provincial authority within; the other is the external building up of the powers of supranational thinking and institutions.

Supranationalism
Man has placed himself, in evolutionary terms, in a doubly unique position. In past aeons species either became extinct because of the overwhelming power of a hostile species or environment or survived by the adaptive process of natural selection. Mankind alone now has the power of both autonomous extinction and autonomous evolution; of all life forms, man alone has control over his own destiny. Abhorrence at the futility and inhumanity of war has turned men's attention to schemes of international collaboration on a number of occasions in the past — witness the paper plans of eighteenth-century philosophers like Kant and the limited reality of Woodrow Wilson's League of Nations. Only in the past generation, however, has man developed the power to destroy civilisation, the whole of mankind, even the totality of life itself. Consciousness of the horror of this potential has concentrated many minds wonderfully on the urgency of global cooperation to prevent war. Of all major thinkers of the early thermonuclear age, Bertrand Russell was particularly vocal in demanding a strategy for survival.

> It seems indubitable [he wrote] that scientific man cannot long survive unless all the major weapons of war, and all the means of mass extermination, are in the hands of a single Authority, which, in consequence of its monopoly, would have irresistible power.... This, it seems plain, is an indispensable condition of the continued existence of a world possessed of scientific skill.[25]

Earlier, he had surveyed mankind's incredible achievements, and cried out:

> Is all this to end in trivial horror because so few are able to think of Man rather than this or that group of men? Is our race so destitute of wisdom, so incapable of impartial love, so blind even to the simplest dictates of self-preservation, that the last proof of its silly cleverness is to be the extermination of all life on our planet?[26]

Since Russell campaigned for nuclear disarmament and a supranational political authority, we, like Dr Strangelove, have learned how to live with the Bomb. But — only to be confronted with predictions of a massive global ecological collapse in the quite foreseeable future. Population explosion, exhaustion of resources of food and raw materials, draining of energy resources, widespread pollution of the environment, seem to interlock into a pattern of inexorable disaster, forged, like the thermonuclear sword of Damocles, by the exquisite skills of scientific and technological man. [27] Again, nothing short of collaboration on a global scale seems likely to divert the planet from its disaster course.

Yet even while listening to these Job-like voices men persist in policies and ways of thinking that are inimical to the collaboration that seems so vital. We are faced, indeed, with a highly paradoxical situation. Technology has now forced mankind by virtual global miniaturisation into greater interdependence than ever before in history, yet politically we live in an era of fragmentation with a rapid multiplication of the number of independent units. The continuing virility of nationalism as a political force has already been demonstrated, bolstered by the notion of sovereignty which defends the concentration of power in the organs of the nation-state. The analogy of Hobbes's vision of the state of nature has frequently been made, the war of all against all: like mankind before the creation of a civil society, nations today live in a condition of lawlessness, the dominant emotion being fear. Fear's close cousin is aggression. When men are afraid they become violent; societies fight wars. But can we risk wars in contemporary society? Is it not possible to calm international fears, reinforce international trust and channel man's aggressive instincts against the environmental perils that, ultimately, endanger the security or even survival of all men?

Many examples of man's capacity for supranational collaboration in practical operations could be cited as grounds for believing that a number of techniques are already developing that are guiding the world to greater cohesion. First, and probably most important, are the multifarious tasks which go on every day on a global scale. Few people pause to give these activities much thought: they none the less bring large numbers of people of different nations into fundamental cooperation. Industry, trade and holidays all take place now with decreasing consciousness of national frontiers, made possible by the communications revolution and leading to greater mutual understanding. A considerable amount of functional cooperation occurs under the aegis of UNO through its Specialised Agencies, like the World Health Organisation, the Food and Agriculture Organisation, and the United Nations International Children's Emergency Fund. Indeed, it could well be argued that supranationalism is more effectively promoted by these activities than by the work of the core political institutions. Nevertheless, and this is the second example of current cooperation, UNO does exist as a primitive political framework for supranational developments. And there are many people who believe that some form of world government is ultimately essential. Advocates of a fully fledged world political order point to the need for an executive authority to take the initiative on a global scale, for a body of world law to which all mankind would be subject and a world force to ensure compliance with this law-based authority. The analogy of the gradual assertion of royal law and order over autonomous local lords in the Middle Ages is often cited. A universally accepted code of law is perhaps the key since a world authority must know what law it is administering and enforcing. The Declaration of Human Rights provides a working basis. The agreement already reached on the exploration and use of outer space and the hoped-for treaty regulating the development of the ocean beds indicate the (albeit slow) progress that is being made in this sphere.

The most notable surrender of national sovereignty has occurred in the creation of the European Economic Community. It is indeed possible that, to come to our third example, the world is moving towards regional groupings of this kind rather than complete global cohesion. [28] The relationship between such partial supranationalism and schemes for total global unity is a matter of hot debate. Some commentators see them as a useful, even essential, first step to a world authority, which would emerge as a global federation of regional federations. Regional federations of this kind have been described as "pillars of a world community" likely "to succeed where the United Nations, based as it is on the jealously guarded national sovereignty of the member states, has inevitably failed". [29] This view may be contrasted with the opinion expressed quite bluntly that "these plans for a European federation ... have nothing whatever to do with world government", [30] because the regional authorities will be so anxious to consolidate their own power. The reader may take his choice.

The potential for futher practical collaborative ventures to erode national boundaries is clearly immense. Yet, like physicists striving to reach in practice the theoretically known temperature of absolute zero, the more steps that are taken towards world unity, the more difficult further progress becomes. The point is that the final breakthrough is dependent not upon a change of technique but on a change of mind. In the words of Einstein in 1946: "The unleashed power of the atom has changed everything except our ways of thinking. . . . We shall require a substantially new manner of thinking if mankind is to survive." [31] The difference between the pragmatic and the theoretical approach is the difference between internationalism and supranationalism, the difference between nations cooperating and a feeling among individuals of belonging to a world community. If supranationalism is to replace nationalism it is necessary to combine the gradual evolution of functional economic and political cooperation with the imaginative ideological leap that will render mankind above all else conscious of his humanity.

If a change of heart is to be effected on this enormous scale, it entails a daunting educational programme — though it is a programme that Unesco has embraced. Again, just as there are the alternatives institutionally of moving directly from national to global organs of power or indirectly via systems of regional federations, so there are similar alternatives in the sphere of concepts of loyalty. One may argue, with Camus, that "little is to be expected from present-day governments, since these live and act according to a murderous code", and conclude that, "men must therefore, as individuals, draw up among themselves, within frontiers and across them, a new social contract which will unite them according to more reasonable principles". [32] On the other hand, and perhaps more realistically, one may conceive, as did John XXIII in his encyclical *Pacem in Terris,* a multi-allegiance system, individuals enjoying a range of identities within a network of loyalties including a global one.

By what routes can man reach a consciousness of the universal in himself? Three major ways may be discerned. First, there is the way of historical consciousness. Marxism is one sidepath of this road, teaching as it does by the lessons of historical inevitability that the state will wither away and leave a classless society as the ultimate product of historical processes. In less specifically ideological terms, one may posit with the nationalist that a shared sense of identity is dependent upon a shared historical consciousness. A sense of supranational loyalty must therefore be nourished by an understanding of universal history, namely of that history which displays the collective experience of mankind rather than the discrete national, even nationalist histories that have been studied in the past. Secondly, there is the path of religion, which in many faiths teaches the brotherhood of man and the consequent ethic of social cohesion and responsibility. Finally, there is the biological route — the recognition that man is a single species. The religious and biological ways to global consciousness have been combined by one of the most original contributors to supranational thought, Teilhard de Chardin. The whole force of the evolutionary process as designed by God, he argued, is directing man into ever closer practical collaboration and, particularly, into thought processes that are universally shared. Human thought, the highest function of evolution and stretching like a membrane over the whole planet, generates an inevitable cosmopolitanism in man. The evolutionary process of Teilhard, like the historical process for Marx, is inevitable:

> How can we fail to see that after rolling us on individually — all of us, you and me — upon our selves, it is still the same cyclone (only now on the social scale) which is still blowing over our heads, driving us together into a contact which tends to perfect each one of us by linking him organically to each and all his neighbours? [33]

It is at least a comfortable thought.

6 The Nature and Importance of Political Ideas

What is the good of political theory?
Politics is concerned with nothing else but the acquisition and retention of power. Whether by election or coup d'état, popular policies or repression – the methods may differ but the ends are the same: power for the politicians. Thus runs the argument of the hardbitten cynic. Of course, power – he may admit – is not pursued nakedly, even though some politicians' clothes are remarkably like the emperor's. No, the seeking after power is tastefully draped in such attractive garments as equality, justice, and law and order. The ability to wield authority over others, to control the destinies of millions of men, women and children, is the ambition that impels the politician; and to achieve his ambition he is willing to admit to principles which he is ready to renounce at will, befriend allies whom he will deny when they are inconvenient, propound policies which he will ignore when they are embarrassing. All that is honourable is sacrificed at the altar of power. Politics is a necessary evil: government we must have, but the process is a dirty business. This, for many people, is the reality of politics. Political theory? All waffle about ideals which have no correspondence with the rough-and-tumble of reality.

This hard cynicism about the actual life of politics has been reinforced by an academic trend away from the study of political philosophy. Political philosophy – the work of the giants like Plato, Locke and Rousseau – is concerned with value-judgments about human nature and society; reasonings about how society *ought* to be arranged, rather than objective facts about how it is. In recent times scholars, especially in the USA, have striven to transform the study of politics into a science. To achieve this end it has been thought necessary that the scholar should be clinical in the acquisition of data, avoiding with utmost scrupulousness any contamination by his personal views. The job of the political scientist is to distinguish between correct and incorrect information, not to judge an institution or a society on a good/bad scale. The emphasis has thus been placed on the collection of information, like a physicist or chemist, in order to understand political phenomena, the function of theory being relegated to the provision of hypotheses and frameworks in order the better to comprehend the mass of material rather than the setting up of normative standards against which to judge political reality. This, it is believed, has been the method whereby the physical sciences have progressed: the social sciences can develop only by following their example.

Moreover, it has been declared, it is about time that politics was weaned away from the great all-embracing ideologies that have sought to explain and mould human society and which have generated such fanaticism and such human misery in our own century. Thus the tenor of the great academic "end of ideology" debate which we shall examine below.

The arguments are, then, that political ideas can and should be dispensed with. But we do so at the risk of impairing our understanding of the political process. For ideas embrace both concepts and values, both of which go far to shape our understanding and action. Concepts determine our perceptions; values determine our priorities. Misunderstandings may well arise through failure to recognise what one's perceptions are: do your concepts of sovereignty and power, for example, accord with mine? Having clarified our concepts we must then be clear about what we wish to be done, and this depends on the kind of society we think is worthwhile. Can the political scientist, can the ordinary citizen, really investigate social institutions and behaviour with the detachment of a physicist investigating the behaviour of subatomic particles? Are not facts and values, in the last analysis, inextricably mixed in the human "sciences"? Put epigrammatically by Bernard Crick: "Politics embodies an ethic and a conscious purpose which cannot be reduced to sociology." And again, "All ideas seek institutional realisation; all institutions embody purposes." [1] Professor Charles Taylor has gone further and argued that where fact and value have traditionally been considered logically distinct, in the field of politics they become intertwined: "A given framework of explanation in political science tends to support an associated value position, secretes its own norms for the assessment of politics and policies." [2]

Let us therefore recognise openly that political activity and the study of political activity cannot be undertaken in a way that totally insulates evidence from points of view, facts from theory. However vigorously the empirical political scientist tries to brush away the value judgments from his study, some fragments will always adhere. Facts must be collected as impartially as possible, certainly. But the questions that are asked and the way the facts are collated will depend on values held by the investigator. Ideas and values are expressed throughout a wide span of sophistication. They appear as slogans and public opinion at the most concrete level. As I write, in the summer of 1972, the five dockers imprisoned for contempt of the Industrial Relations Court are said by supporters to have been as unjustly sentenced as the Tolpuddle Martyrs. This is a political judgment based on the belief that the Industrial Relations Act (or certain portions of it) is politically vindictive. At the opposite, abstract end of the spectrum are the great classical formulations of ideas like Natural Law and the General Will. The range of really basic political ideas is quite limited. They are founded on simple attitudes about human nature and society: whether man can be entrusted with more or less freedom, whether the individual or society should be given prior consideration, what are the legitimate bases and the extent of political authority. In the long run it is one's response to such issues that determines one's political response. The issues are raised in different circumstances at different times and in different societies. The detailed experience changes; the fundamental values are perennial.

This is not to say that attitudes and opinions are always necessarily consciously held. Most folk react in political ways, by voting or formulating an opinion about a crisis situation such as a strike, without even recognising that facts and values can be distinguished, that their view is coloured perhaps by the newspaper they read or their socio-economic status or the education they have received. But because political ideas are not consciously recognised as such, it does not mean that they are not there. Political ideas permeate the whole of civilised society, even if *The Leviathan* is not to be found on everyone's bedside table.

The end of ideology debate
It is noticeable that major works of political theory, like, for example, *The Leviathan* are no longer being produced. Scholars started to point

out this phenomenon in the 1950s. However, the debate among the academics became very complex and confused. There was little agreement on either the exact nature of the phenomenon or its causes. Alfred Cobban, out of the mainstream of the debate but probably more acute in his analysis, noted the failure of our age to produce thinkers of the calibre of Hobbes, Rousseau and Marx. In the past, he wrote, "the flow of ideas has been punctuated at intervals by the synthesis created by a great political thinker. No such synthesis has appeared in our own day or for some time past".[3] He diagnosed a hiatus in original creative thinking. This was rather different from the great debate entered into largely by American political scientists, who discussed the phenomenon they described as "the end of ideology".[4] But even within this camp there was confusion, some arguing the total end of all ideological thinking, others that what had come to an end was the production of great, all-embracing, apocalyptic ideologies. Yet others preferred to talk of a *decline* in ideology (with the likelihood of its revivification) rather than an end. Moreover, whatever was the precise nature of the phenomenon being observed, commentators were divided as to whether the development was beneficial or detrimental to human wellbeing.

Those who rejoiced at the perceived end or decline in ideology have emphasised the beneficence of consensus and the growing affluence, in the West at least, that has drained politics of intense conflict. Grand ideological designs have been proved worse than useless; they introduced emotion and fanaticism into political behaviour in the 1930s. The world has now learned to live without this totalitarian intensity and is a better place for it. In the words of Daniel Bell:

> Few serious minds believe any longer that one can set down "blueprints" and through "social engineering" bring about a new utopia of social harmony. At the same time, the older [liberal] "counter-beliefs" have lost their intellectual force as well. . . . In the Western world, therefore, there is today a rough consensus among intellectuals on political issues.[5]

Not all the participants in the debate were quite so sanguine. If theorising about politics was at a discount, overshadowed by the search for scientific facts, this revealed an unfortunate shift of emphasis from ends to a means — renunciation of the ethical function of politics, a replacement of the good by the workable. This was viewed as either an unfortunate temporary displacement or a disastrous truncation of a vital feature of European thought. A vision of the good society, however unattainable in any total sense, had acted as a beacon, affording men a sense of direction in their political journeyings. Bereft of an ideal, as Ortega y Gasset observed, men will drift: "We live at a time when man believes himself fabulously capable of creation, but he does not know what to create. Lord of all things, he is not lord of himself. The world today goes the same way as the worst of worlds that have been: it simply drifts." [6]

On the other hand, the view that political theorising has come to a dead end has not been universally accepted. There is the view, expressed by Crick and Taylor already cited, that theory and practice cannot be divorced, either logically or functionally. Political life and political study are inconceivable without the adoption of value positions. Indeed, has not this present book revealed a flurry of theorising, of action based on ideological considerations? It would be strange indeed to finish a book on contemporary political ideas by concluding that they are non-existent; by reducing the substance of its chapters to mere shadows.

What are we, then, to conclude? The academics have tried to turn the subject into a science. But this is of minor significance. What is important is that theory has not kept pace with fact. Like a once-proud city that has not been adapted to the changing demands of twentieth-century urban life, our stock of political ideas has a shabby, decayed, rather derelict appearance. Vast grand theories of history probably are dangerous. But we do need a framework of values shaped to the conditions of our time — not the nationalism, utilitarian liberalism and Marxism of a former age repainted and passed off for new.

Political socialisation

Political ideas are diffused through a society as the opinions, attitudes and beliefs of its citizens. But how are these opinions, attitudes and beliefs acquired and developed? In some countries a deliberate policy of indoctrination is undertaken — the activities of Goebbels in Nazi Germany is an obvious example of such an approach. In most states the process is much more subtle, indirect and complex. We are constantly subjected to influences that help to determine both our basic and our more detailed political orientations. We hear our parents and friends talk, we pick up opinions from the television and newspapers. Every individual has to learn in some way to adapt to the system in which he is living and every system, if it is to remain stable, has to encourage this process of adaptation. In a famous study, Gabriel Almond and Sidney Verba have termed a successful participatory relationship between the citizen and the government as the civic culture. In summing up how this relationship is established they provide a succinct description of the way in which people learn to fit into the system — the process of political socialisation, as it is called:

> The civic culture is transmitted by a complex process that includes training in many social institutions — family, peer group, school, work place, as well as in the political system itself. Furthermore, the types of experience within these institutions vary. Individuals learn political orientations through intentional teaching, as in a school civics class; but they also learn through overtly political experiences that are not intended to be lessons in politics, as when the child overhears parents discussing politics, when he observes the actions of the political system. Or the training in political orientations may be neither explicit nor political in content, as when the individual learns about authority from participating in authority structures in the family or the school or when he learns about the trustworthiness of others from his early contact with adults. [7]

It is not suggested that these influences define an individual's political attitude for all time, but rather that they give him a predisposition to certain political stances. The socialisation process will affect a person's tendency to support or reject the system as a whole, shape his determination to engage in political activity like voting and influence his party allegiance.

Family influence is clearly the most pervasive since it operates intensively and continuously over a long period of time. Studies have indicated that the family has a considerable effect in shaping a person's attitude towards authority in general and in providing a party identification. W.S. Gilbert may have stretched things a bit when he wrote:

> I often think it's comical
> How Nature always does contrive
> That every boy and every gal,
> That's born into the world alive,
> Is either a little Liberal,
> Or else a little Conservative. [8]

Indeed, political sociologists reject this implied *inheritance* of political views in favour of the acquisition of attitudes through environmental influences, of which the family is the most significant. Nevertheless, Gilbert intuitively displayed a shrewd understanding of the early adoption of party allegiance that has been supported by modern research. For example, Mark Abrams has shown that in the early 1960s 70 per cent of the children of Conservative fathers and 60 per cent of children of Labour fathers followed their parents' party commitment. [9] Education, however, is believed to be important more for its level than its content. [10] And this is connected, too, with a person's socio-economic status. The more highly educated and the more socially secure a person is the more likely he is to participate in political activity and feel that he can have some effect.

The question of education raises the matter of the age at which people acquire political attitudes. It has frequently been assumed that politics is an adult activity beyond the comprehension and interest of young people. Nevertheless, a considerable amount of research, especially in the USA, has shown that basic attitudes, often admittedly very crudely understood and formulated, are already taking shape in the minds of children of even junior school age. [11] An investigation in Leeds in 1969, for example, showed that "at the beginning of secondary school, nine out of ten children have a definite party commitment". Though "when we matched their party affiliations with their knowledge of party policies, there was no correlation: Labour or Conservative were labels, no different in kind from brand names of soap". [12] But the point here is not the accuracy or sophistication of young people's political opinions. The important conclusion from this research is that the adult citizen has been moulded by his childhood experiences, probably without realising it.

Readers of this book might well look to themselves. As the motto on the temple of Delphi advised: γνῶθι σεαυτόν — know thyself. One should be conscious of one's opinions and recognise one's prejudices. And an effective way of achieving this is to test one's attitude about a significant and currently newsworthy incident against the views of parents, friends, teachers and newspapers. Are your views vague or defined? How do they compare with these other sources of opinion? How influenced have you been by them? Why do you hold the views you do?

How to decide

Knowing one's own mind, being politically literate, is particularly important in the contemporary world. It is important for the recognition of political danger signals. Perhaps the rights of the individual are being endangered by creeping bureaucratic technocracy; if so, the values that are threatened and the perils that loom should be fully and widely appreciated. It is important also for intelligent participation in the political process and the exercise of judicious choice. In order to accomplish this it is necessary to penetrate the smokescreen of slogans and media-processing that often cloaks the true ideas and motives of politicians and parties, not to mention the skill that is required to make a responsible choice from the cacophony of voices peddling a bewildering variety of political wares.

This exercise takes the form of identifying one's position on the Right – Left spectrum. [13] The terminology originated in the French assembly because the radicals tended to cluster on the benches to the left of the president's chair and the conservatives to the right. The left is identified with the ideal of popular sovereignty with consequent emphasis on liberty, social reform and change. The Right is identified with respect for tradition, the established order and change only by evolutionary growth. In many ways, therefore, the distinction marks a fundamental cleavage in political attitudes. In practice, there has developed a whole spectrum of political colours, shading from one to the other from ultra-blue reactionaries to infra-red revolutionaries. A simplified model would read as follows: Fascism-Conservatism-Liberalism-Socialism-Communism. The linear spectrum is still the most widely used model though it is clearly not an absolutely accurate representation of reality. For example, it does not explain the totalitarian tendencies which the extreme *ends* of the spectrum have *in common*. To meet this difficulty, Professor Eysenck has proposed a two-dimensional model, plotting radical-conservative along one axis and "tender-mindedness" and "tough-mindedness" along the other. [14] It is an interesting refinement and worthy of investigation, but it has not gained general currency.

Faced with a set of political ideas or a programme, what questions should one pose in order to test their validity and to arrive at a responsible judgment? We may produce a convenient checklist of five major questions. Firstly, what are the priorities in a civil society? Justice, freedom, efficiency, stability and progress are all deemed desirable by most people. But they may not be comparable. We need to know how these are balanced in any doctrine or programme; and if the subordination of some ideals in favour of others is not made explicit we need to probe more deeply to ask where the catch is. If freedom and efficiency or stability and progress are mutually incompatible, which is to be sacrificed and by how much? These issues are absolutely basic to any society.

In the second place, one needs to ask what should be the relative emphasis given to the ideal and the possible? One needs an ideal as a yardstick against which to test policies, as a goal to aim for, to provide a sense of purpose and direction. Nevertheless, it is possible to be impractically dogmatic. It is necessary to trim and tack before the contrary winds of ideological and pragmatic criticism. But again, by how much, before one finds oneself blown completely off course?

Thirdly, what is the correct balance between the rights of the individual and the needs of society? Does the full flowering of the individual personality have prior claim or should society be viewed as an organic whole whose total requirements must take precedence over individual whims? Again, where should the balance lie? How much can individuals be justly allowed to suffer for the good of society as a whole? Or, indeed, need there be any clash of interests — can we not achieve a correspondence between the requirements of the individual and of society?

Fourthly, it is necessary to judge the accuracy of the factual basis and the coherence of the logical argument of the doctrine or programme. If it is founded on inaccurate data or faulty arguments, one needs to assess how seriously the whole structure is thereby undermined.

And finally, one must distinguish between the rational and emotional appeal of a doctrine. One must not be deceived into supporting a programme for supposedly rational reasons when the appeal is in fact emotional. This is not to condemn emotion out of hand. In truth it is a dangerous quality in politics — leading to fanaticism and intolerance. Yet it is necessary if one is to respond to a programme with a convinced commitment.

There is nothing in the world of politics quite so important as ideas. They grip the imagination, evoke the strength of purpose that comes from faith and thus provide the motive force for all significant political action. The citizen has no more arduous and no more responsible task than to subject the programmes that are purveyed by the politicians and demonstrators to the most vigorous enquiry; to investigate their fundamental ideas and ensure that they are good.

Notes and References

Chapter 1 The Shaping of Contemporary Political Ideas

1. For a masterly survey of twentieth-century ideas, see Anthony Quinton, "Ideas and Beliefs", in Alan Bullock, ed., *The Twentieth Century* (Thames and Hudson, 1971).
2. Isaiah Berlin, "Political Ideas in the Twentieth Century" (1950), reprinted in *Four Essays on Liberty* (Oxford University Press, 1969), p. 39.

Chapter 2 Mainstream Ideas in Britain

1. R.T. McKenzie, *British Political Parties* (Heinemann, 1955), p. 586.
2. Samuel H. Beer, *Modern British Politics* (Faber, rev. edn, 1969), pp. 387-8.
3. Speech, 5 December 1957, quoted in Peter Mansfield, *Nasser's Egypt* (Penguin 1965), p. 136.
4. Quoted in Basil Davidson, *Which Way Africa?* (Penguin, 1964), p. 17.
5. A.H. Hanson, "The Future of the Labour Party", *The Political Quarterly*, vol. 41 no. 4 (1970), p. 378
6. Beer, *op. cit.,* p. 108
7. Hugh Gaitskell, "Public Ownership and Equality", *Socialist Commentary*, June 1958, reprinted in Frank Bealey, *The Social and Political Thought of the British Labour Party* (Weidenfeld & Nicolson, 1970), p. 198.
8. The Labour Party's Manifesto for the 1970 General Election, p. 14.
9. Quoted in Paul Foot, *The Politics of Harold Wilson* (Penguin, 1968), p. 123.
10. Beer, *op. cit.,* p. 135.
11. Quoted in Foot, *op. cit.,* p. 138.
12. Reprinted in Henry Pelling, *The Challenge of Socialism* (A. and C. Black, 1954), p. 330.
13. See below, pp. 51-4.

14. Reprinted in F.W.S. Craig, ed., *British General Election Manifestos, 1918-1966* (Political Reference Publications, 1970), p. 234.
15. The Labour Party's Manifesto, 1970.
16. The Labour Party's Manifesto for the 1959 general election, reprinted in Craig, *op. cit.*, p.197.
17. R.H.S. Crossman in *New Fabian Essays* (1952), reprinted in Pelling, *op. cit.*, p. 349.
18. Reprinted in Craig, *op. cit.*, p. 101.
19. Beer, *op. cit.*, p. 149.
20. Speech at Birmingham, 19 January 1964, reprinted in *The New Britain: Labour's Plan* (Penguin, 1964), pp. 14-5.
21. See Peter Sedgwick, "Varieties of Socialist Thought", In Bernard Crick and William A. Robson, eds., *Protest and Discontent* (Penguin, 1970).
22. Quintin Hogg, *The Case for Conservatism* (Penguin, 1947), pp.12 and 14.
23. Peter Shore, *The Real Nature of Conservatism* (1952), quoted in Beer, *op. cit.*, p. 249n.
24. The Conservative Party's Manifesto for the 1950 General Election, reprinted in Craig, *op. cit.*, p. 126.
25. R.J. White, *The Conservative Tradition* (A. and C. Black, 1950), p. 3.
26 The Conservative Party's Manifesto for the 1970 Election, p. 30.
27. Esmond Wright, "The Future of the Conservative Party", *The Political Quarterly*, vol. 41, no. 1 (1970), p. 389.
28. Quoted *ibid.*, p. 392.
29. L.S. Amery, *Thoughts on the Constitution* (1953), quoted in Beer, *op. cit.*, p. 96.
30 Hogg, *op. cit.*, p. 11.
31. T.R. Fyvel, *The Insecure Offenders* (1961), quoted in D. Thomson, *England in the Twentieth Century* (Penguin 1965), p. 261.
32. Michael Oakeshott, "On Being Conservative", reprinted in *Rationalism in Politics and Other Essays* (Methuen, 1962), p. 192.
33. Nigel Harris, *Beliefs in Society* (Penguin, 1971), p. 114.
34. Quoted in Roy Douglas, *The History of the Liberal Party, 1895-1970* (Sidgwick & Jackson, 1971), p. xvi.
35. Preamble to the Liberal Party constitution, quoted *ibid.*, p. 297.
36. The Liberal Party Manifesto for the 1966 General Election, reprinted in Craig, *op. cit.*, p. 293.
37. *Liberals Look Ahead,* quoted in *The Guardian,* 27 August 1969.
38. *ibid.*
39. Bernard Crick, *In Defence of Politics* (Penguin, 1964), p. 123.
40. Alan Bullock and Maurice Shock, *The Liberal Tradition* (A. and C. Black, 1956), p. liv.

Chapter 3 Ideological Panaceas

1. David Easton, *A Systems Analysis of Political Life* (Wiley, 1965), p. 290.
2. Isaac Deutscher, *Marxism in Our Time* (Cape, 1972), p. 16.
3. Karl Marx and Friedrich Engels, *Communist Manifesto* (ed. Harold Laski Allen & Unwin, 1948), pp. 119-21.
4. Speech on 1 July 1958, quoted in Dieter Dux, *Ideology in Conflict: Communist Political Theory* (Van Nostrand, 1963), p. 12.
5. *The British Road to Socialism,* 1951; third rev. edn, 1968.
6. *ibid.,* p. 5.
7. Resolution adopted by the congress of the Communist International, quoted in G.H. Sabine, *A History of Political Theory* (Harrap, 3rd edn, 1951), p. 674.
8. *The British Road to Socialism,* p. 22.
9. Arthur Koestler in R.H.S. Crossman, ed., *The God That Failed* (Hamish Hamilton, 1950), p. 68
10. Kenneth Newton, *The Sociology of British Communism* (Allen Lane, 1969), p. 154.
11. *Communist Manifesto,* p. 160.
12. *The British Road to Socialism,* p. 48.
13. L. Trotsky, *The Permanent Revolution,* reprinted in C. Wright Mills, *The Marxists* (Penguin, 1963), p. 274.
14. Speech, 13 March 1967, quoted in David Horowitz, *Imperialism and Revolution* (Penguin, 1971), p. 227.
15. Quoted in Z.A.B. Zeman, *Prague Spring: a Report on Czechoslovakia 1968* (Penguin, 1969), pp. 117 and 122.
16. V.I. Lenin, *Left-Wing Communism, an Infantile Disorder,* quoted in Newton, *op. cit.,* p. 16.
17. *The British Road to Socialism,* p. 56.
18. *Ibid.,* p. 6.
19. *Quotations from Chairman Mao Tse-tung* (Foreign Languages Press, Peking, 1966), p. 200.
20. *The Wretched of the Earth* (Penguin, 1967), p. 74
21. Herbert Marcuse, *Eros and Civilisation* (1955), quoted in Maurice Cranston, "Herbert Marcuse", in Maurice Cranston, ed., *The New Left* (Bodley Head, 1970), p. 97.
22. Andrew Sinclair, *Guevara* (Fontana/Collins, 1970), p. 65.
23. Quoted in George Feaver, "Black Power" in Cranston, *op. cit.,* p. 154.
24. Quoted in Philip Mason, *Race Relations* (Oxford University Press, 1970), p. 97.
25. Reprinted in Louis L. Snyder, *The Idea of Racialism* (Van Nostrand, 1962), p. 133.
26. Nicholas Deakin, *Colour, Citizenship and British Society* (Panther, 1970), p. 33.

27. See W.W. Daniel, *Racial Descrimination in England* (Penguin, 1968) and Gus John and Derek Humphry, *Because They're Black* (Penguin, 1971).
28. Chief Kaiser Matanzima, quoted in A. Hepple, *Verwoerd* (Penguin, 1967), p. 190.
29. See Ronald Segal, *The Race War* (Penguin, 1967).
30. "Huey Newton Talks to *The Movement*" in Richard P. Young, *Roots of Rebellion* (Harper & Row, 1970), pp. 383-4.
31. Quoted in Paul Foot, *The Rise of Enoch Powell* (Penguin, 1969), p. 38.
32. *The Times*, first leader, 27 May 1968.
33. Charles Reich, *The Greening of America* (1970), quoted in Raymond Williams, *Politics and Technology* (Macmillan, 1971), p. 36.
34. C.P. Snow, *Science and Government* (Oxford University Press, 1961), p. 1.

Chapter 4 Organisation Within the Political Unit

1. *The Politics*, Bk. III, chs. vi-viii.
2. Paul Goodman, *Anarchy*, no. 96, February 1969, quoted in April Carter, *The Political Theory of Anarchism* (Routledge & Kegan Paul, 1971), pp. 9-10.
3. P. Kropotkin, *Anarchism: Its Philosophy and Ideal*, quoted in Carter, *op. cit.*, pp. 51-2.
4. Jerry Rubin, *We are Everywhere* (1971), quoted in James M. Glass, "'Yippies': the Critique of Possessive Individualism"; *The Political Quarterly*, 43, no. 1 (1972).
5. See Chapter 4 pp. 73-8.
6. Quoted in Norman F. Cantor, *The Age of Protest* (Allen & Unwin, 1969), p. 274.
7. Quoted in Bernard Crick, *In Defence of Politics* (Penguin, 1964), p. 41.
8. *Quotations from Chairman Mao Tse-tung* (Foreign Languages Press, 1966), p. 299.
9. George Orwell, *Animal Farm* (1945; Penguin edn, 1951), p. 80.
10. Quoted in Hannah Arendt, *The Origins of Totalitarianism* (Allen & Unwin, 1958), p. 455.
11. V. Tarsis, *Ward 7* (Collins and Harvill Press, 1965), pp. 27-8.
12. Joseph Schumpeter, *Capitalism, Socialism and Democratic Theory* (Cambridge University Press, 1970), p. 4.
13. Quoted in Henry Fairlie, *The Life of Politics* (Methuen, 1968), p. 16.
14. For a splendidly full historical analysis of the political cohesion of the Atlantic area at the genesis of modern democracy, see R.R. Palmer, *The Age of the Democratic Revolution* (Princeton

University Press, 1959 and 1964).
15. C.B. Macpherson, *The Real World of Democracy* (Oxford University Press, 1966). p. 16.
16. *Ibid.*, p. 35.
17. Reprinted in Walter Consuelo Langsam, *Historic Documents of World War II* (Van Nostrand, 1958), p. 66.
18. Isaiah Berlin, "Two Concepts of Liberty", reprinted in *Four Essays on Liberty*, (Oxford University Press, 1969), p. 171.
19. Bernard Crick, "Toleration and Tolerance in Theory and Practice", *Government and Opposition*, vol. 6, no. 2 (1971), p. 144.
20. H.B. Mayo, *An Introduction to Democratic Theory* (1960), quoted in Dorothy Pickles, *Democracy* (Methuen, 1970), p. 155.
21. See below, pp. 75-76.
22. Alfred Cobban, *In Search of Humanity* (Cape, 1960), p. 103.
23. Walter Bagehot, *The English Constitution*, quoted in Pickles, *op. cit.*, p. 147.
24. For a succinct summary of the process in Europe and America, see Geoffrey Barraclough, *An Introduction to Contemporary History* (Watts, 1964), chap. 5.
25. For a discussion of these two principles as operated in Britain, see Chapter 2.
26. See below, pp. 76-77.
27. R.H. Tawney, *Equality* (1931), quoted in Pickles, *op. cit.*, p. 62.
28. Pateman, *op. cit.*, p. 1.
29. Bernard Crick, " 'Them and Us': Public Impotence and Government Power" (Gaitskell Memorial Lecture 1968), reprinted in *Political Theory and Practice* (Allen Lane, 1972).
30. See, for example, Erich Fromm, *The Fear of Freedom* (Routledge & Kegan Paul, 1942).
31. Julius Nyerere, *Democracy and the Party System* (1963), quoted in Basil Davidson, *Which Way Africa?* (Penguin, 1964), p. 111.
32. Robert Kilroy-Silk "Contemporary Theories of Industrial Democracy", *The Political Quarterly*, vol. 41, no. 2 (1970).
33. *In Place of Strife: A Policy for Industrial Relations* (Cmnd 3888, HMSO, 1969), para. 19, quoted *ibid.*
34. Pateman, *op. cit.*, p. 102.
35. Macpherson, *op. cit.*, pp. 21 and 32.
36. See Bernard Crick, "A Defence of Politics against Democracy", in *In Defence of Politics* (Penguin,1964).

Chapter 5 Organisation of the Political Unit

1. Quoted in Elie Kedourie, *Nationalism* (Hutchinson, 1961), p. 73.
2. This feature of nationalism is not very well covered in the literature on the subject, but see K.W. Deutsch, *Nationalism and Social Communication*, 2nd edn. (M.I.T. Press, 1966).

118 Contemporary Political Ideas

3. Hugh MacDiarmid in O.D. Edwards *et al., Celtic Nationalism* (Routledge & Kegan Paul, 1968), pp. 321-2.
4. See p. 83 above.
5. Dadalshi Naoroji, *Condition of India: Correspondence with the Secretary of State for India,* quoted in Elie Kedourie, *Nationalism in Asia and Africa,* (Weidenfeld & Nicolson, 1970), p. 355.
6. Jean-Paul Sartre, Preface to Frantz Fanon, *The Wretched of the Earth* (Penguin, 1967), p.19. Fanon is too important a figure to be dismissed so briefly. His ideas are treated more fully in the section on the New Left in Chapter 3.
7. See the section on Racialism in Chapter 3.
8. For a fuller discussion of this development, see below, pp. 95-7.
9. See above, pp. 81-2. The belief that *racial* differences are of political significance is dealt with under the separate heading of Racialism in Chapter 3. In many ways the two phenomena are expressions of similar feelings.
10. For a fuller discussion of the historical dimension, see below, pp. 93-4.
11. From the Italian *irredentista,* unredeemed.
12. Kwame Nkrumah, *Ghana Today,* 26 April 1961 quoted in Colin Legum, *Pan-Africanism,* (Praeger, 1962), p. 66.
13. Liam de Paor, *Divided Ulster* (Penguin, 1971), p. xiii.
14. MacDiarmid, *op. cit.,* p. 331.
15. Quoted in Kedourie, *Nationalism* p. 106.
16. See Chapter 4.
17. This tendency leads ultimately to totalitarianism. See Chapter 4.
18. Lord Acton, "Nationality", in *Essays on Freedom and Power,* (Thames & Hudson, 1956, edn.), p. 168.
19. The term "provincialism" has been used rather than "regionalism", the frequently used word, in order to avoid confusion with multi-national federalism, also often referred to as regionalism.
20. See above, pp. 88-9.
21. Committee on the Management of Local Government, 1967 quoted in J.P. Mackintosh, *The Devolution of Power,* Penguin, 1969, pp. 28-9.
22. Mackintosh, *op. cit.,* p. 100.
23. Gwynfor Evans and Ioan Rhys in Edwards *et al., op. cit.,* p. 289.
24. See, for example, John Pinder and Roy Pryce, *Europe After de Gaulle,* (Penguin, 1969).
25. Bertrand Russell, *Has Man a Future?* (Penguin, 1961), p. 71.
26. Bertrand Russell, *Portraits from Memory* (1956) quoted in Peter Mayer, ed., *The Pacifist Conscience* (Penguin, 1966), pp. 321-2.
27. For a discussion of the relationship between science and politics, see Chapter 3.
28. See the references to the pan-movements above, pp. 90-1.
29. Pinder and Pryce, *op. cit.,* pp. 158-9.

30. L.J. Cohen, *The Principles of World Citizenship* (Blackwell, 1954), p. 100.
31. Quoted in Otto Klineberg, *The Human Dimension in International Relations* (Holt, Rinehart & Winston, 1964), p. 155.
32. Albert Camus, "Neither Victims nor Executioners" (1946) quoted in Mayer, *op. cit.,* pp. 435-6.
33. Pierre Teilhard de Chardin, *The Phenomenon of Man* (Collins/ Fontana, Eng. trans. 1959), p. 334.

Chapter 6 The Nature and Importance of Political Ideas

1. Bernard Crick, *In Defence of Politics* (Penguin, 1964), pp. 172 and 199.
2. C. Taylor, "Neutrality in Political Science", in Peter Laslett and Walter G. Runciman, eds., *Philosophy, Politics and Society,* third series (Blackwell, 1967), p. 184.
3. Alfred Cobban, "The Decline of Political Theory" (1953), reprinted in *France Since the Revolution and Other Essays on Modern History* (Cape, 1970), p. 191.
4. For a definition of the term "ideology", see above, pp. 26-7.
5. Daniel Bell, *The End of Ideology* (Free Press, rev, edn., 1962), p. 402.
6. Ortega y Gassett, *The Revolt of the Masses* (1932), quoted in Cobban, *op. cit.,* p. 191.
7. Gabriel A. Almond and Sidney Verba, *The Civic Culture* (Princeton University Press, 1963), pp. 498-9.
8. W.S. Gilbert, *Iolanthe,* Act I.
9. Cited in W. Gardner, "Political Socialization". in Derek Heater, ed., *The Teaching of Politics* (Methuen, 1969), pp. 37-8.
10. See, for example, Seymour Martin Lipset, *Political Man* (Heinemann, 1960), pp. 55-6.
11. See, for example, F. Greenstein, *Children and Politics* (Yale University Press, 1965).
12. T.J. Nossiter, "How Children Learn about Politics", *New Society,* 31 July 1969.
13. For a discussion of the operation of the Right-Left model in Britain, see Chapter 2 above. For a discussion of the problems of accurate definition, see David Caute, *The Left in Europe Since 1789* (Weidenfeld & Nicolson, 1966), Part I.
14. H.J. Eysenck, "Politics and Personality", in *Sense and Nonsense in Psychology* (Penguin, 1957).

Select Bibliography

Here are a mere twenty-eight references selected from a vast possible range. They represent a mixture of readings, broad analyses and depth studies, chosen to lead the reader beyond the superficiality of the present volume. Titles published in paperback are marked with an asterisk.

Chapters 1 The Shaping of Contemporary Political Ideas and 6 The Nature and Importance of Political Ideas.

Crick, B. *In Defence of Politics,* Penguin, 1964*
A succinct, lively, thought-provoking analysis of the reality of politics based on the premise that its essence is conciliation. Should be read by all who find the present book too elementary.
Quinton, A. "Ideas and Beliefs", in A. Bullock, ed., *The Twentieth Century,* Thames & Hudson, 1971.
Not confined to *political* ideas, but a brilliant cameo of the intellectual history of the present century, placing political thinking in this general setting.
Utley, T.E. and Maclure, J.S., *Documents of Modern Political Thought,* Cambridge University Press, 1957.
Rather old now and each extract is only a scrap, but it is still useful as an introduction to the primary sources of the main threads of contemporary political thought.

Chapter 2 Mainstream Ideas in Britain

Bealey, F. *The Social and Political Thought of the British Labour Party,* Weidenfeld & Nicolson, 1970.
A chronological approach. Major documents and speeches have been judiciously selected and a clear introductory essay sets the scene admirably.
Beer, S.H., *Modern British Politics,* rev. edn., Faber, 1969*

A masterly transatlantic view of the evolution and present condition of the British parties, but mercifully free of transatlantic jargon. He argues a thesis cogently, dealing with much more than ideas. A "must" for students of British politics, though he is stronger on Socialism than Conservatism.

Craig, F.W.S., ed., *British General Election Manifestos 1918-1966,* (Political Reference Publications, 1970. An invaluable reference book for finding out what the three major parties promised.

Hogg, Q., *The Case for Conservatism* Penguin, 1947*

Dated in its partisanship, but a vigorous and thorough exposition of the Conservative credo with both historical and (then) contemporary references. Hence, not too abstract.

Chapter 3 Ideological Panaceas

The British Road to Socialism, British Communist Party, 3rd edn., 1968. The official party manifesto.

Cranston, M., ed., *The New Left,* Bodley Head, 1970.

A series of disconnected essays, not particularly sympathetic to the movement. But a useful summary of the ideas of the main exponents.

Horowitz, D. *Imperialism and Revolution*, Penguin, 1971*

A left-wing view of the Cold War. He includes a useful up-to-date pro-Marx, anti-Stalin exposition of Communism.

Hudson, G.F., *Fifty Years of Communism,* Watts, 1968; also Penguin*

A history of Communism since the Russian Revolution in a rightish nutshell. Quite basic, not for the sophisticated student.

Mason, P., *Race Relations,* Oxford University Press, 1970*

An extremely useful little book by the former Director of the Institute of Race Relations. It manages to pack in an incredible amount of material (biological, psychological, historical, etc.) in a very small compass without talking down to the reader.

Segal, R., *The Race War,* Penguin, 1967*

A pessimistic, panoramic view of race relations throughout the world. You may not agree with him in the end, but you will have learned a lot en route. A large book, packed with information. Sympathetic to the coloured races.

Snow, C.P., *Science and Government* Oxford University Press, 1961

Developing his famous "two cultures" thesis, Lord Snow, in these equally famous Godkin lectures, shows how serious ignorance of science in government circles can be.

Williams, R., *Politics and Technology,* Macmillan, 1971*

Rather indigestible. A highly condensed summary of the vast literature on the subject. At least it is quicker than going to the originals and therefore a handy introduction.

Wright Mills, C. *The Marxists,* Penguin, 1963*

A collection of extracts with explanatory material ranging from Marx to Che Guevara, compiled by the late master left-wing sociologist. A useful introduction to a vast political literature.

Chapter 4 Organisation within the Political Unit

Arendt, H., *The Origins of Totalitarianism*, 2nd edn., Allen & Unwin, 1958.

A massive, erudite study of this terrifying phenomenon. Most readers of the present book will not have the time to cope with the whole of Miss Arendt's work, but great profit may be derived from Part III (chs. 10-14).

Carter, A. *The Political Theory of Anarchism*, Routledge & Kegan Paul 1972.

Many books on anarchism concentrate heavily on the nineteenth century. This is analytical in approach and takes its illustrative material from the present century also. Quite short.

Macpherson, C.B., *The Real World of Democracy,* Oxford University Press, 1966*

A series of brief lectures arguing that liberal democracy is but one of three forms of government that might justifiably lay claim to the title. The Marxism is not *too* obtrusive.

Mason, P.T., *Totalitarianism: Temporary Madness or Permanent Danger?* Heath, 1967*

A collection of readings (plus a very brief introduction) from over twenty authorities. One of the "Problems in European Civilization" series.

Pateman, C., *Participation and Democratic Theory,* Cambridge University Press, 1970.

A most thoughtful discussion of this most relevant of modern issues. Demanding in a scholarly way, it is well worth reading — especially for those interested in "the nature of democracy" questions.

Pickles, D.,*Democracy,* Methuen, 1970*

A most judicious, simple-yet-scholarly and up-to-date survey of democracy in theory and practice. Illustrations are drawn from Britain, USA and France. A very good introduction to the subject.

Chapter 5 Organisation of the Political Unit

Edwards, O.D., *et al., Celtic Nationalism*, Routledge & Kegan Paul, 1968
Three uneven essays, spatchcocked together — uneven in style, length and approach to the subject, the section on Ireland being very historical. Useful for bringing the countries of the Celtic fringe together in one volume.

Kedourie, E. *Nationalism,* Hutchinson, 1961*
A little masterpiece. Historical, theoretical and pessimistic. Well worth the effort of concentration by anyone interested in the subject.

Kedourie, E., *Nationalism in Asia and Africa* Weidenfeld & Nicolson, 1970.
A most useful companion to the previous title. Apart from the geographical limitation, this book is different in being less abstract. The bulk of the volume consists of extracts, but there is an equally useful and thorough introduction.

Mackintosh, J.P., *The Devolution of Power,* Penguin, 1968*
Somewhat dated already, but it contains useful ideas on decentralisation for Great Britain simply expounded by a professor-politician.

Minogue, K., *Nationalism,* Methuen, 1969*
A simpler, more narrative introduction to the subject for those who find Professor Kedourie's book of the same title too heavy-going.

Russell, B., *Has Man a Future?* Penguin, 1961*
There is no really good single book on supranationalism. This is rather dated and idiosyncratic, but still worth pondering on.

Index